AN EXCERPT FROM

HEBREWS

(CHAPTER 11:1-40)

THE
PREACHER'S
OUTLINE & SERMON
BIBLE®

NEW TESTAMENT

NEW INTERNATIONAL VERSION

Leadership Ministries Worldwide
PO Box 21310
Chattanooga, TN 37424-0310
www.lmw.org

The Preacher's Outline & Sermon Bible® is written for God's people to use in their preparation for preaching and teaching. Leadership Ministries Worldwide wants God's people to use **The Preacher's Outline & Sermon Bible**®. The purpose of the copyright is to prevent the reproduction, misuse, and abuse of the material.

May our Lord bless us all as we preach, teach, and write for Him, fulfilling His great commission to make disciples of all nations.

Previous Editions of **The Preacher's Outline & Sermon Bible**®,
King James Version,
Copyright © 1991, 1996
by Alpha-Omega Ministries, Inc.

Please address all requests for information or permission to:
LEADERSHIP MINISTRIES WORLDWIDE
1928 Central Avenue
Chattanooga, TN 37408
Ph.# (423) 855-2181   FAX (423) 855-8616
E-Mail: info@lmw.org
http://www.lmw.org

Library of Congress Catalog Card Number: 96-75921
International Standard Book Number: 978-1-57407-141-2

Printed in the United States of America

LEADERSHIP MINISTRIES WORLDWIDE

DEDICATED

To all the men and women of the world who preach and teach the Gospel of our Lord Jesus Christ and to the Mercy and Grace of God

&

- Demonstrated to us in Christ Jesus our Lord.

  In him we have redemption through his blood, the forgiveness of sins, in accordance with the riches of God's grace. (Ep.1:7)

- Out of the mercy and grace of God, His Word has flowed. Let every person know that God will have mercy upon him, forgiving and using him to fulfill His glorious plan of salvation.

  For God so loved the world that he gave his one and only Son, that whoever believes in him shall not perish but have eternal life. For God did not send his Son into the world to condemn the world, but to save the world through him. (Jn.3:16-17)

  This is good, and pleases God our Savior, who wants all men to be saved and to come to a knowledge of the truth. (1 Ti.2:3-4)

6/10

The Preacher's Outline & Sermon Bible®

is written for God's servants to use in their study, teaching, and preaching of God's Holy Word...

- to share the Word of God with the world.
- to help believers, both ministers and laypersons, in their understanding, preaching, and teaching of God's Word.
- to do everything we possibly can to lead men, women, boys, and girls to give their hearts and lives to Jesus Christ and to secure the eternal life that He offers.
- to do all we can to minister to the needy of the world.
- to give Jesus Christ His proper place, the place the Word gives Him. Therefore, no work of Leadership Ministries Worldwide—no Outline Bible Resources—will ever be personalized.

OUTLINE BIBLE RESOURCES

This material, like similar works, has come from imperfect man and is thus susceptible to human error. We are nevertheless grateful to God for both calling us and empowering us through His Holy Spirit to undertake this task. Because of His goodness and grace, *The Preacher's Outline & Sermon Bible*® New Testament and the Old Testament volumes are now complete.

The Minister's Personal Handbook, The Believer's Personal Handbook, and other helpful **Outline Bible Resources** are available in printed form as well as releasing electronically on various software programs.

God has given the strength and stamina to bring us this far. Our confidence is that as we keep our eyes on Him and remain grounded in the undeniable truths of the Word, we will continue to produce other helpful Outline Bible Resources for God's dear servants to use in their Bible Study and discipleship.

We offer this material, first, to Him in whose name we labor and serve and for whose glory it has been produced and, second, to everyone everywhere who studies, preaches, and teaches the Word.

Our daily prayer is that each volume will lead thousands, millions, yes even billions, into a better understanding of the Holy Scriptures and a fuller knowledge of Jesus Christ the Incarnate Word, of whom the Scriptures so faithfully testify.

You will be pleased to know that Leadership Ministries Worldwide partners with Christian organizations, printers, and mission groups around the world to make Outline Bible Resources available and affordable in many countries and foreign languages. It is our goal that *every* leader around the world, both clergy and lay, will be able to understand God's Holy Word and present God's message with more clarity, authority, and understanding—all beyond his or her own power.

LEADERSHIP MINISTRIES WORLDWIDE
1928 Central Avenue • Chattanooga, TN 37408
(423) 855-2181 FAX (423) 855-8616
info@lmw.org
www.lmw.org – FREE download materials
6/16

ACKNOWLEDGEMENTS

Every child of God is precious to the Lord and deeply loved. and every child as a servant of the Lord touches the lives of those who come in contact with him or his ministry. The writing ministry of the following servants have touched this work, and we are grateful that God brought their writings our way. We hereby acknowledge their ministry to us, being fully aware that there are so many others down through the years whose writings have touched our lives and who deserve mention, but the weaknesses of our minds have caused them to fade from memory. May our wonderful Lord continue to bless the ministry these dear servants, and the ministry of us all as we diligently to labor to reach the world for christ and to meet the desperate needs of those who suffer so much.

THE GREEK SOURCES

1. Expositor's Greek Testament, Edited by W. Robertson Nicoll. Grand Rapids, MI: Eerdmans Publishing Co., 1970.

2. Robertson, A.T. Word Pictures in the New Testament. Nashville, TN: Broadman Press, 1930.

3. Thayer, Joseph Henry. Greek-English Lexicon of the New Testament. New York: American Book Co., No date listed.

4. Vincent, Marvin R. Word Studies in the New Testament. Grand Rapids, MI: Eerdmans Publishing Co., 1969.

5. Vine, W.E. Expository Dictionary of New Testament Words. Old Tappan, NJ: Fleming H. Revell Co., No date listed.

6. Wuest, Kenneth S. Word Studies in the Greek New Testament. Grand Rapids, MI: Eerdmans Publishing Co., 1966.

THE REFERENCE WORKS

7. Cruden's Complete Concordance of the Old & New Testament. Philadelphia, PA: The John C. Winston Co., 1930.

8. Josephus' Complete Works. Grand Rapids, MI: Kregel Publications, 1981.

9. Lockyer, Herbert. Series of Books, including his books on All the Men, Women, Miracles, and Parables of the Bible. Grand Rapids, MI: Zondervan Publishing House, 1958-1967.

10. Nave's Topical Bible. Nashville, TN: The Southwestern Co., No date listed.

11. The Amplified New Testament. (Scripture Quotations are from the Amplified New Testament, Copyright 1954, 1958, 1987 by the Lockman Foundation. Used by permission.)

12. The Four Translation New Testament (Including King James, New American Standard, Williams - New Testament In the Language of the People, Beck - New Testament in the Language of Today.) Minneapolis, MN: World Wide Publications.

13. The New Compact Bible Dictionary, Edited by T. Alton Bryant. Grand Rapids, MI: Zondervan Publishing House, 1967.

14. The New Thompson Chain Reference Bible. Indianapolis, IN: B.B.Kirkbride Bible Co., 1964.

THE COMMENTARIES

15. Barclay, William. Daily Study Bible Series. Philadelphia, PA: Westminister Press, Began in 1953.

16. Bruce, F.F. The Epistle to the Ephesians. Westwood, NJ: Fleming H. Revell Co., 1964.

17. Bruce, F.F. Epistle to the Hebrews. Grand Rapids, MI: Eerdmans Publishing Co., 1964.

18.   Bruce, F.F. <u>The Epistles of John</u>. Old Tappan, NJ: Fleming H. Revell Co., 1970.

19.   Criswell, W. A. <u>Expository Sermons on Revelation</u>. Grand Rapids, MI: Zondervan Publishing House, 1962-66.

20.   Greene, Oliver. <u>The Epistles of John</u>. Greenville, SC: The Gospel Hour, Inc., 1966.

21.   Greene, Oliver. <u>The Epistles of Paul the Apostle to the Hebrews</u>. Greenville, SC: The Gospel Hour, Inc., 1965.

22.   Greene, Oliver. <u>The Epistles of Paul the Apostle to Timothy & Titus</u>. Greenville, SC: The Gospel Hour Inc., 1965.

23.   Greene, Oliver. <u>The Revelation Verse by Verse Study</u>.. Greenville, SC: The Gospel Hour, Inc., 1963.

24.   Henry, Matthew. <u>Commentary on the Whole Bible</u>. Old Tappan, NJ: Fleming H. Revell Co.

25.   Hodge, Charles. <u>Exposition on Romans & on Corinthians</u>. Grand Rapids, MI: Eerdmans Publishing Co., 1972-1973.

26.   Ladd, George Eldon. <u>A Commentary on the Revelation of John</u>. Grand Rapids, MI: Eerdmans Publishing Co., 1972-1973.

27.   Leupold, H.C. <u>Exposition of Daniel</u>. Grand Rapids, MI: Baker Book House, 1969.

28.   Morris, Leon. <u>The Gospel According to John</u>. Grand Rapids, MI: Eerdmans Publishing Co., 1971.

29.   Newell, William R. <u>Hebrews, Verse by Verse</u>. Chicago, IL: Moody Press, 1947.

30.   Strauss, Lehman. <u>Devotional Studies in Galatians & Ephesians</u>. Neptune, NJ: Loizeaux Brothers, 1957

31.   Strauss, Lehman. <u>Devotional Studies in Phillipians</u>. Neptune, NJ: Loizeaux Brothers, 1959.

32.   Strauss, Lehman. <u>James, Your Brother</u>. Neptune, NJ: Loizeaux Brothers, 1956.

33.   Strauss, Lehman. <u>The Book of the Revelation</u>. Neptune, NJ: Loizeaux Brothers, 1964.

34.   <u>The New Testament & Wycliffe Bible Commentary</u>. Edited by Charles F. Pfeiffer & Everett F. Harrison. New York: The Iverson Associates, 1971. Produced for Moody Monthly. Chicago Moody Press, 1962.

35.   <u>The Pulpit Commentary</u>, Edited by H.D.M. Spence & Joseph S. Exell. Grand Rapids, MI: Eerdmans Publishing Co., 1950.

36.   Thomas W.H. Griffith. <u>Hebrews, A Devotional Commentary</u>. Grand Rapids, MI: Eerdmans Publishing Co., 1970.

37.   Thomas W.H. Griffith. <u>Outline Studies in the Acts of the Apostles</u>. Grand Rapids, MI: Eerdmans Publishing Co., 1956.

38.   Thomas W.H. Griffith. <u>St. Paul's Epistle to the Romans</u>. Grand Rapids, MI: Eerdmans Publishing Co., 1970.

39.   Thomas W.H. Griffith. <u>Studies in Colossians & Philemon</u>. Grand Rapids, MI: Eerdmans Publishing Co., 1970.

40.   <u>Tyndale New Testament Commentaries</u>. Grand Rapids, MI: Eerdmans Publishing Co., Began in 1958.

41.   Walker, Thomas. <u>Acts of the Apostles</u>. Chicago, IL: Moody Press, 1965.

42.   Walvoord, John. <u>The Thessalonian Epistles</u>. Grand Rapids, MI: Zondervan Publishing house, 1973.

*"Woe is unto me, if I
preach not the gospel"*
(1 Co.9:16)

		mended as a righteous man, when God spoke well of his offerings. And by faith he still speaks, even though he is dead.	a. Illust. by Abel: The power to be counted righteous
	CHAPTER 11 **D. The Description of Faith, 11:1–6**		b. Illust. by Enoch: The power to walk with God & to be delivered from death
1 The meaning of faith a. Being sure of one's hope b. Being certain of the unseen **2 The reward of faith: God's approval** **3 The basic understanding of faith: God made the world** **4 The spiritual power of faith**	Now faith is being sure of what we hope for and certain of what we do not see. 2 This is what the ancients were commended for. 3 By faith we understand that the universe was formed at God's command, so that what is seen was not made out of what was visible. 4 By faith Abel offered God a better sacrifice than Cain did. By faith he was com-	5 By faith Enoch was taken from this life, so that he did not experience death; he could not be found, because God had taken him away. For before he was taken, he was commended as one who pleased God. 6 And without faith it is impossible to please God, because anyone who comes to him must believe that he exists and that he rewards those who earnestly seek him.	**5 The necessary beliefs of faith**[DS1] a. Must believe that God exists b. Must believe that God rewards the earnest seeker

DIVISION IV

THE SUPREME AUTHOR OF FAITH: JESUS CHRIST, GOD'S SON, 10:19–11:40

D. The Description of Faith, 11:1–6

(11:1–6) **Introduction:** this is one of the great chapters in the Bible. It is known as *God's Great Hall of Fame*. Men and women who have *believed* God down through the centuries are listed as being great men and women of God. The key to greatness with God is faith; the person who truly believes God is *great* in the eyes of God. The key to any of us being great in the eyes of God is faith—faith in God's Son, the Lord Jesus Christ. The first part of this great chapter gives us an overall study of faith. It is the *description of faith*.

1. The meaning of faith (v. 1).
2. The reward of faith: God's approval (v. 2).
3. The basic understanding of faith: God made the world (v. 3).
4. The spiritual power of faith (v. 4–5).
5. The necessary beliefs of faith (v. 6).

1 (11:1) **Faith**: the meaning of faith. What does faith mean? This is the only time the Bible ever defines faith. Time and time again, the Bible discusses faith and the great importance of faith. The Bible tells us that we must have faith—we must believe God—and it tells us the great things that happen to those who do believe God. The Bible also gives example after example of men and women who have and have not believed God and shows in clear terms what happened to each. But nowhere does the Bible define faith except here. Thus it is important that we clearly see just what faith means. The Biblical definition is this (see Heb.11:1 in each of the following author's commentaries for their discussion):

"Now faith is the substance of things hoped for, the evidence of things not seen" (v. 1).

"Now faith is the assurance of things hoped for, the conviction of things not seen" (v. 1, New American Standard).

"Now faith is the assurance of the things we hope for, the proof of the reality of the things we cannot see" (v. 1, Williams).

"Faith is being sure of the things we hope for, being convinced of the things we can't see" (v. 1, Beck).

"Now faith is the assurance (the confirmation, the title-deed) of the things [we] hope for, being the proof of things [we] do not see and the conviction of their reality—faith perceiving as real fact what is not revealed to the senses" (v. 1, Amplified New Testament).

"Now faith is the title deed of things hoped for, the conviction of things which are not being seen" (Kenneth Wuest).

"Faith means that we are certain of the things we hope for, convinced of the things we do not see" (William Barclay).

"Faith is a hope that is absolutely certain that what it believes is true, and that what it expects will come" (Barclay says this is what faith is to the writer of Hebrews).

"Faith is trust in the unseen. It is not trust in the unknown, for we may know by faith what we cannot see with the eye" (Wycliffe Bible Commentary).

"Faith apprehends as a real fact what is not revealed to the senses. It rests on the fact, acts upon it, and is upheld by it in the face of all that seems to contradict it. Faith is a real seeing" (Marvin Vincent).

"Faith is the substance, the foundation, the title deed, the assurance of things hoped for" (Oliver Greene).

That great servant of God of a former generation whom so many appreciate so much, Matthew Henry, makes some excellent statements that are well worth our thought:

"Faith and hope go together; and the same things that are the object of our hope are the object of our faith.

"It [faith] is a firm persuasion and expectation that God will perform all that He has promised to us in Christ; and this persuasion is so strong that it gives the soul ... possession ... of those things.

"Believers in the exercise of faith are filled with joy unspeakable and full of glory. Christ dwells in the soul by faith; and the soul is filled with the fullness of God."

Now, what is faith? Look at the Biblical definition again.

Now faith is being sure of what we hope for and certain of what we do not see. (v. 1)

The word "sure" (hupostasis) means the foundation, assurance, title-deed, and guarantee of things hoped for. The word "certain" (elegchos) means conviction.

According to most commentators, this is what is meant by these two words. Therefore, faith would be defined as:

"Now faith is the assurance of things hoped for, the conviction of things not seen."

Look closely at what is being said and note that faith is being described as an act, an act of the mind and heart. That is, our heart and mind believe something and we have assurance and conviction that it is true. This is certainly true; faith is an act of the mind and heart. But many of the earlier interpreters understood "sure" (hupostasis) to mean *real being, substantial nature, the real nature of a thing.* Vincent points this out and even says that it suggests the real sense, but he backs off of the meaning and concludes that faith is basically an act of what he calls "moral intelligence directed at an object" (*Word Studies In The New Testament*, Vol. 4, p. 510).

This is not to argue with God's dear servants who stress that faith is primarily an act of the mind and heart. It is only to say that Scripture seems to be saying that faith is more than an act. Scripture seems to be saying that faith is the *actual possession* of reality. Is this not what the definition "title-deed" is saying? The person who holds the title-deed to property actually possesses the property. It is his already. Certainly from God's perspective, we already possess His promises; He has already seated us in the heavenlies, and we already possess eternal life. It is not that we are going to possess it; we already possess it. The point is this: holding the title-deed to property and possessing something is more than assurance and conviction. It is possessing reality, actually holding something that is substantial and real. It is possessing the land, the promises of God. Faith is possessing the substance of the promises of God, the actual evidence of things not seen. If I possess them, the substance is there; the evidence is there. The substance and evidence, the fact that I already possess them, are my assurance and conviction. This is important to note and bears repeating: the substance and evidence, the fact that I already possess eternal life, is the basis of my assurance and conviction, of never tasting and experiencing death.

Now, what does all this discussion mean? It means this: faith is *being sure, the actual possession,* of what we hope for, the *certainty and reality* of what we do not see. It is *both an act and a possession* of the thing believed. It is believing and trusting in that which actually exists—in that which we can possess. We may not be able to see it, but it is real and exist-

ing, and we can possess it by believing and having faith in it. We can possess it now—we cannot see it, but we can actually possess the very substance of it by believing and entrusting our lives to it.

- ☞ Faith is *trusting and possessing* all that God is and says.
- ☞ Faith is *believing and possessing* all that God is and says.
- ☞ Faith is *having confidence in and possessing* all that God is and says.
- ☞ Faith is *hoping for something and possessing it* because God exists and has promised it.

Thought 1. Note what Biblical faith is not. It is not...
- "I think so, I hope so."
- "It may be so; it may not be so."
- "It might be true; it might not be true."

Biblical faith does not deal with what is unreal, imaginary, fanciful, visionary, superficial, or deceptive. Biblical faith is the knowledge, experience, and possession of things hoped for. True Biblical faith deals only with truth and reality. It is...
- knowing what is real.
- experiencing what is real.
- possessing what is real.

2 (11:2) **Faith:** the reward of faith. What is the reward of faith? God's approval. God is pleased, very pleased, when we believe Him and His promises. This is the point of this verse. The elders, great men of God who lived in the past, believed God and followed God. They turned away from the world and its possessions and pleasures and followed God. They believed God, that He had much more to offer—that His promises of an eternal land and of eternal life were true. Therefore they staked their lives, all they were and had, upon that hope. And their faith in God pleased God to no end. Therefore, God accepted their faith and has honored them because of it. He has, of course, honored them by recording their faith in His Word and using their example as a challenge to believers of every generation. But God has also honored them by fulfilling their faith; God has taken them on home to be with Him.

Thought 1. The reward of faith is God's approval, and when God approves us, He accepts us into His eternal presence. This simply means that God looks after and cares for us, giving us victory over all the enemies of this world—including death—and He does it for eternity. The approval of God means that God fulfills all His promises to us. The promises of God become a living reality in our experiences, both daily and eternally.

That everyone who believes in him may have eternal life. "For God so loved the world that he gave his one and only Son, that whoever believes in him shall not perish but have eternal life. (John 3:15–16)

"I tell you the truth, whoever hears my word and believes him who sent me has eternal life and will not be condemned; he has crossed over from death to life. (John 5:24)

He came to Derbe and then to Lystra, where a disciple named Timothy lived, whose mother was a Jewess and a believer, but whose father

was a Greek. The brothers at Lystra and Iconium spoke well of him. (Acts 16:1–2)

First, I thank my God through Jesus Christ for all of you, because your faith is being reported all over the world. (Rom. 1:8)

And we are sending along with him the brother who is praised by all the churches for his service to the gospel. (2 Cor. 8:18)

To the praise of his glorious grace, which he has freely given us in the One he loves. In him we have redemption through his blood, the forgiveness of sins, in accordance with the riches of God's grace (Eph. 1:6–7)

Demetrius is well spoken of by everyone— and even by the truth itself. We also speak well of him, and you know that our testimony is true. (3 John 1:12)

3 (11:3) **Faith—Creation:** the basic understanding of faith—that God has made the world. Note the word "understanding" (noeo). It means to perceive with the mind, to understand, to know a true fact. Some say the belief that God made the world is only an assumption, that it is the beginning point in building the Christian's beliefs and theology. There is both truth and error in this charge. The error is found in the word assumption. The truth is this: the Christian begins with a fact that is true: *God did create the world.* The Christian believer's starting point is more than an assumption—it is an understanding, a true fact, the very basic fact that God did create the world. This understanding is based upon four things:

- ✏ The world itself: looking at and observing the world, and studying and thinking about its origin, purpose, and end.
- ✏ The Bible, the Word of God, the written revelation of God.
- ✏ The Lord Jesus Christ, the living revelation of God.
- ✏ The witness of the Holy Spirit who is given to every believer. He bears witness that Jesus Christ and the Word of God are true. This is critical, for it is a fact, as any true Christian believer can testify. When a per son believes in the Lord Jesus Christ, God puts His Spirit into the heart and life of the deliverer. The Holy Spirit seals, guarantees, bears witness that Jesus Christ is the Son of God and that the promises and teachings of God's Word are true.

The point is this: the Christian believer has four strong sources that show the origin, purpose, and end of all things; and all four are undeniable. How can this be said? How can we say that these witnesses are undeniable?

- ✏ Because we can look and observe the world. The world is real; it is truth. The world does exist.
- ✏ Because we can look and observe the Bible, its teachings and promises at work in human lives—the lives of those who believe it. The Word of God sitting there and working itself out in lives is real. The Word of God is truth; it is absolutely true that it exists and works in human lives just as it claims.
- ✏ Because we can know the Lord Jesus Christ through a study of the records of His life. He lived, and the fact that He lived is truth. But we can also see that the very things He claimed are at work in human lives. Jesus Christ can be studied and known in the lives of those who truly believe and follow Him. For Jesus

Christ lives in the lives of true believers and followers of His.

- ✏ Because we can know and see the work of the Holy Spirit in lives as discussed above.

Again, the believer has four strong witnesses that testify that God exists—that He exists and that He has created the worlds. Where did the worlds come from? A chart is probably the best way to grasp what the believer understands as opposed to what the unbeliever understands.

When a believer looks at the origin of the world, he sees …
1. God
2. God's Word—God willed and spoke
3. Matter appeared, the worlds were created by God's Word
4. The things seen were made by God

When an unbeliever looks at the origin of the world, he sees …
1. Nothing—absolutely nothing
2. Nothing—absolutely nothing
3. Matter appeared; some gas or force formed out of absolutely nothing
4. The things seen were made by just appearing out of absolutely nothing

The point is this: we were not here when God created the world, but we *believe* that a Supreme Being, God Himself, created the world.

- ✏ The world says that a Designer made the world.
- ✏ The Bible, the Word of God, says that God made the world.
- ✏ Jesus Christ says that God made the world.
- ✏ The Holy Spirit testifies to the believer's heart that the claims and promises of the Word of God are true.

Therefore, the basic understanding of the believer is that God exists and that He has created the world. God is the Person who is behind life and the world of life. God gave breath to man and His world. He made the things that are seen.

Thought 1. Matthew Henry has an excellent exposition on this point that merits our study.

"By faith we understand much more of the formation of the world than ever could be understood by the naked eye of natural reason. Faith is not a force upon the understanding, but a friend and a help to it. Now what does faith give us to understand concerning the worlds? …

1. That these worlds were not eternal, nor did they produce themselves, but they were made by another.

2. "That the maker of the worlds is God: he is the maker of all things.

3. "That he made the world with great exactness; it was a framed work, in everything duly adapted and disposed to answer its end.

4. "That God made the world by his word, that is, by his essential wisdom and eternal Son, and by his active will, saying, Let it be done, and it was done, Ps. 33.

5. "That the world was thus framed out of nothing, out of no pre-existent matter … [by] God, who can call things that are not as if they were, and command them into being. These things we understand by faith.

"The Bible gives us the truest and most exact account of the origin of all things, and we are to believe it, and not to wrest or run down the scripture-account of the creation, because it does not suit with some fantastic hypotheses of our own, which has been in some learned but conceited men the first remarkable step towards infidelity, and has led them into many more" (Matthew Henry's Commentary, Vol. 6, p. 938).

Thought 2. William Barclay also has his usual practical comments that are helpful in the personal application of this point to our lives.

"The writer to the Hebrews goes further. He says that it is an act of faith to believe that God made this world. Then he goes on to say that the things which are seen emerged from the things which are not seen. Now when he said that he was aiming a blow at current belief. It was current belief that God created the world out of already existing matter, and not out of nothing. Further, it was current belief that this existing matter was flawed and that therefore from the beginning this is a flawed world because it is made from flawed material. The writer to the Hebrews insists that God did not work with existing material; God created the world from nothing. Now when he argued like this he was not interested in cosmological speculation. He was not interested in the scientific side of the matter. What he wanted to stress was the fact that this is God's world. If we can grip the fact that this is God's world, that God is responsible for it, then two things follow. First, we will use it as such. We will remember that everything in it is God's and we will try to use it as God would have us use it. Second, we will remember that, even when it does not look like it, somehow God is in control. If we believe that this is God's world then there comes the faith and the hope which enable us to do the most difficult thing in the world—to accept what we cannot understand. If we believe that this is God's world then into life there comes a new sense of responsibility and into life there comes a new power of acceptance, for everything belongs to God, and all is in the hands of God" (The Letter to the Hebrews, p. 147f).

In the beginning God created the heavens and the earth. (Gen. 1:1)

You alone are the LORD. You made the heavens, even the highest heavens, and all their starry host, the earth and all that is on it, the seas and all that is in them. You give life to everything, and the multitudes of heaven worship you. (Neh. 9:6)

He spreads out the northern skies over empty space; he suspends the earth over nothing. (Job 26:7)

For he founded it upon the seas and established it upon the waters. (Psa. 24:2)

By the word of the LORD were the heavens made, their starry host by the breath of his mouth. (Psa. 33:6)

The sea is his, for he made it, and his hands formed the dry land. (Psa. 95:5)

In the beginning you laid the foundations of the earth, and the heavens are the work of your hands. (Psa. 102:25)

He set the earth on its foundations; it can never be moved. (Psa. 104:5)

When they heard this, they raised their voices together in prayer to God. "Sovereign Lord," they said, "you made the heaven and the earth and the sea, and everything in them. (Acts 4:24)

Has not my hand made all these things?' (Acts 7:50)

"Men, why are you doing this? We too are only men, human like you. We are bringing you good news, telling you to turn from these worthless things to the living God, who made heaven and earth and sea and everything in them. (Acts 14:15)

By faith we understand that the universe was formed at God's command, so that what is seen was not made out of what was visible. (Heb. 11:3)

4 (11:4–5) **Faith, Power of—Abel—Enoch—Cain:** the spiritual power of faith. The power of faith is the message of the glorious gospel, the glorious hope that God has given from the beginning of time. The power is twofold and it is given in the most meaningful way possible, by showing how the power takes effect in the lives of believers. Two believers who experienced the power of faith were Abel and Enoch.

1. Faith has the power to be counted as righteousness. No greater gift could be given us than to give us the glorious privilege of being counted righteous by God.

⮑ To be counted righteous is the great need of man, for we are not righteous. And unless some way can be found to cause God to count us righteous, we shall never be allowed to live with God.

Abel tells us there is a way to be counted righteous. How? By approaching and worshipping God exactly like He says, that is, by the sacrifice of blood. What does this mean?

When Adam and Eve sinned, they became aware of their nakedness. Nakedness is a symbol of their being aware and conscious of sin (cp. Gen. 3:9–10). God loved them; therefore, He provided clothing to cover their nakedness. Note what the clothing was. It was coats or skins from animals, a symbol that sin had to be covered by the shedding of blood. This was a symbol that pointed to the blood of Jesus Christ, the blood of God's Son, that had to be shed in order to cover the sins of men.

The point is this: from the very first parents on earth, God laid it down that the sin and guilt of man had to be borne by either man himself or by a substitute. Man had to die for his own sins or else a substitute had to be sacrificed for his sins. Adam and Eve taught this to their children. Note what happened.

Adam lay with his wife Eve, and she became pregnant and gave birth to Cain. She said, "With the help of the LORD I have brought forth a man." Later she gave birth to his brother Abel. Now Abel kept flocks, and

Cain worked the soil. In the course of time Cain brought some of the fruits of the soil as an offering to the LORD. But Abel brought fat portions from some of the firstborn of his flock. The LORD looked with favor on Abel and his offering, but on Cain and his offering he did not look with favor. So Cain was very angry, and his face was downcast. Then the LORD said to Cain, "Why are you angry? Why is your face downcast? If you do what is right, will you not be accepted? But if you do not do what is right, sin is crouching at your door; it desires to have you, but you must master it." Now Cain said to his brother Abel, "Let's go out to the field." And while they were in the field, Cain attacked his brother Abel and killed him. (Gen. 4:1–8)

By faith Abel offered God a better sacrifice than Cain did. By faith he was commended as a righteous man, when God spoke well of his offerings. And by faith he still speaks, even though he is dead. (Heb. 11:4)

The difference between the two offerings was this: Abel believed God and approached and worshipped God exactly as God said: through the sacrifice of another, the sacrifice of an animal. But Cain did not believe God. He did not accept God's Word; he did not approach God through the sacrifice of another. He made a material sacrifice and offering to God: he approached God through money and earthly gifts, through the efforts and fruits of human works, the fruit borne of the earth, the fruit borne by his own human, frail, aging, and dying hands.

Very simply, Abel believed God. He recognized just what Scripture says: that he was sinful and imperfect and that he could never be acceptable to God who is perfect and holy, not until his sins and their guilt had been paid for and removed. Abel knew that his sins had to be removed—that he had to be counted righteous before he could ever be accepted by God. Therefore, he believed God would count him righteous if he let another bear his sins for him. He believed exactly what Scripture proclaims to us.

He himself bore our sins in his body on the tree, so that we might die to sins and live for righteousness; by his wounds you have been healed. (1 Pet. 2:24)

For Christ died for sins once for all, the righteous for the unrighteous, to bring you to God. He was put to death in the body but made alive by the Spirit, (1 Pet. 3:18)

This is the power of faith: faith gives us the power to be counted righteous.

Abram believed the LORD, and he credited it to him as righteousness. (Gen. 15:6)

Through him everyone who believes is justified from everything you could not be justified from by the law of Moses. (Acts 13:39)

For all have sinned and fall short of the glory of God, and are justified freely by his grace through the redemption that came by Christ Jesus. (Rom. 3:23–24)

What does the Scripture say? "Abraham believed God, and it was credited to him as righteousness." (Rom. 4:3)

Therefore, since we have been justified through faith, we have peace with God through our Lord Jesus Christ, (Rom. 5:1)

Since we have now been justified by his blood, how much more shall we be saved from God's wrath through him! (Rom. 5:9)

Because anyone who has died has been freed from sin. (Rom. 6:7)

Who will bring any charge against those whom God has chosen? It is God who justifies. (Rom. 8:33)

And that is what some of you were. But you were washed, you were sanctified, you were justified in the name of the Lord Jesus Christ and by the Spirit of our God. (1 Cor. 6:11)

Know that a man is not justified by observing the law, but by faith in Jesus Christ. So we, too, have put our faith in Christ Jesus that we may be justified by faith in Christ and not by observing the law, because by observing the law no one will be justified. (Gal. 2:16)

Consider Abraham: "He believed God, and it was credited to him as righteousness." (Gal. 3:6)

So the law was put in charge to lead us to Christ that we might be justified by faith. (Gal. 3:24)

And be found in him, not having a righteousness of my own that comes from the law, but that which is through faith in Christ—the righteousness that comes from God and is by faith. (Phil. 3:9)

Thought 1. Note that Cain approached God; he was religious. But his religion was a formal religion:

- ✎ a religion of ritual, form, and ceremony.
- ✎ a religion of personal sacrifice and works, of doing good and even of sacrificing in order to do good.
- ✎ a religion of man, of his own choosing, of his own ideas and imaginations as to how he was to approach God.

What an indictment of so many religions! What a challenge to search our hearts and lives to make sure that we are worshipping God through His own dear Son who died for our sins.

2. Faith has the power to give us a day by day walk with God and to deliver us from death. What a glorious gift: the presence and power of God as we walk day by day and the eternal deliverance from death. Enoch illustrates this:

Enoch walked with God; then he was no more, because God took him away. (Gen. 5:24)

By faith Enoch was taken from this life, so that he did not experience death; he could not be found, because God had taken him away. For before he was taken, he was commended as one who pleased God. (Heb. 11:5)

Enoch believed God, believed that if he walked and fellowshipped with God day by day then God would look after and care for him. Therefore Enoch walked with God and God looked after and cared for him. God even conquered death for Enoch. When Enoch was ready to go home to God, God transferred him right on into heaven, right into God's very own presence. Enoch experienced the promise that is made to every believer: we shall never taste or experience death.

➥ Enoch's faith gave him a day by day walk with God—the knowledge and fellowship, care and provision, protection and deliverance of God.

Remain in me, and I will remain in you. No branch can bear fruit by itself; it must remain in the vine. Neither can you bear fruit unless you remain in me. "I am the vine; you are the branches. If a man remains in me and I in him, he will bear much fruit; apart from me you can do nothing. If anyone does not remain in me, he is like a branch that is thrown away and withers; such branches are picked up, thrown into the fire and burned. If you remain in me and my words remain in you, ask whatever you wish, and it will be given you. (John 15:4–7)

God did this so that men would seek him and perhaps reach out for him and find him, though he is not far from each one of us. (Acts 17:27)

God, who has called you into fellowship with his Son Jesus Christ our Lord, is faithful. (1 Cor. 1:9)

So then, just as you received Christ Jesus as Lord, continue to live in him, (Col. 2:6)

Come near to God and he will come near to you. Wash your hands, you sinners, and purify your hearts, you double-minded. (James 4:8)

We proclaim to you what we have seen and heard, so that you also may have fellowship with us. And our fellowship is with the Father and with his Son, Jesus Christ. (1 John 1:3)

Whoever claims to live in him must walk as Jesus did. (1 John 2:6)

Here I am! I stand at the door and knock. If anyone hears my voice and opens the door, I will come in and eat with him, and he with me. (Rev. 3:20)

The LORD is close to the brokenhearted and saves those who are crushed in spirit. (Psa. 34:18)

The LORD is near to all who call on him, to all who call on him in truth. (Psa. 145:18)

➥ Enoch's faith gave him the longed for deliverance from death.

Just as Moses lifted up the snake in the desert, so the Son of Man must be lifted up, that everyone who believes in him may have eternal life. (John 3:14–15)

"For God so loved the world that he gave his one and only Son, that whoever believes in him shall not perish but have eternal life. (John 3:16)

Whoever believes in the Son has eternal life, but whoever rejects the Son will not see life, for God's wrath remains on him." (John 3:36)

At this the Jews exclaimed, "Now we know that you are demon-possessed! Abraham died and so did the prophets, yet you say that if anyone keeps your word, he will never taste death. (John 8:52)

Now this is eternal life: that they may know you, the only true God, and Jesus Christ, whom you have sent. (John 17:3)

But we see Jesus, who was made a little lower than the angels, now crowned with glory and honor because he suffered death, so that by the grace of God he might taste death for everyone. (Heb. 2:9)

The one who sows to please his sinful nature, from that nature will reap destruction; the one who sows to please the Spirit, from the Spirit will reap eternal life. (Gal. 6:8)

Thought 1. Oliver Greene has an excellent application on Enoch that stirs the glorious hope of conquering death:

"It has been said that Enoch was walking with God one day, and they walked and talked so long in such sweet fellowship that near nightfall God said to Enoch, 'It is nearer to my house than to your house, so let us go on to my house.' That is a wonderful way to think about it, but the Bible simply tells us that 'Enoch walked with God, and was not, for God took him,'

"... the record of Enoch, though very brief, is in a very unique place in the Word of God. In Genesis 5, beginning with verse 5, we read:

'And all the days that Adam lived were nine hundred and thirty years - and he died.'

'And all the days of Seth were nine hundred and twelve years - and he died' (v. 8).

'And all the days of Enos were nine hundred and five years - AND HE DIED' (v. 11).

'And all the days of Cainan were nine hundred and ten years - and he died' (v. 14).

'And all the days of Mahalaleel were eight hundred ninety and five years - and he died' (v. 17).

'And all the days of Jared were nine hundred sixty and two years - and he died' (v. 20).

'And all the days of enoch were three hundred sixty and five years: and Enoch walked with God, and he WAS NOT, FOR GOD TOOK HIM' (vv. 23, 24).

'And all the days of Methuselah were nine hundred sixty and nine years - AND HE DIED' (v. 27).

'And all the days of Lamech were seven hundred seventy and seven years - AND HE DIED' (v. 31).

"From these passages we note that Enoch lived in one of the darkest periods of human history, he lived in the midst of dying men, and yet he did not die. He was translated; God took him to heaven - alive.

"Enoch is definitely a type of the New Testament saints who will be translated when the church is caught up to meet the Lord in the

air, in the midst of an age of wholesale death and in an hour darker than any yet known to man! Surely that hour is upon us. Surely these are the days known as 'the beginning of sorrows.' The darkest hour is always just before dawn, and surely the night is far spent. Surely Jesus will come quickly. We do not know the day or the hour of His coming, but we do believe He is coming soon" (The Epistle of Paul the Apostle to the Hebrews. Greenville, SC: The Gospel Hour, 1965, p. 448f).

5(11:6) **Faith—God, Existence:** the necessary beliefs of faith. This is one of the great verses of Scripture, a verse that should be memorized and held within the heart of every believer, layman as well as minister:

> **And without faith it is impossible to please God, because anyone who comes to him must believe that he exists and that he rewards those who earnestly seek him. (Heb. 11:6)**

1. It is impossible to please God without faith. By faith is meant a living, active faith, a faith that knows and follows God, communes and fellowships with God. It does not matter what a person does; without faith he cannot please God. It is utterly impossible to please God without faith. What does this mean? The person will never be acceptable to God nor accepted by God. Without faith the person will never live with God, not in this world nor in the next world. Without faith, a person has to plow through this life all alone and handle all the trials, temptations, sufferings, accidents, diseases, and death by himself. Without faith, a person stands all alone in this world—utterly without God. It is impossible for him to please God. The Greek scholar Kenneth Wuest says:

> *"The writer lays down an axiomatic truth. He uses the aorist tense in the infinitive 'to please.' The statement is universal in its application and timeless. The idea is, 'Without faith it is impossible to please Him at all'"* (Hebrews, Vol. 2, p. 198).

> **I tell you the truth, we speak of what we know, and we testify to what we have seen, but still you people do not accept our testimony. (John 3:11)**
> **Whoever believes in him is not condemned, but whoever does not believe stands condemned already because he has not believed in the name of God's one and only Son. (John 3:18)**
> **Whoever believes in the Son has eternal life, but whoever rejects the Son will not see life, for God's wrath remains on him." (John 3:36)**
> **I told you that you would die in your sins; if you do not believe that I am the one I claim to be, you will indeed die in your sins." (John 8:24)**
> **See to it, brothers, that none of you has a sinful, unbelieving heart that turns away from the living God. (Heb. 3:12)**

2. The person who comes to God must believe two things.
   a. He *must believe* in God—that God is—that God exists. The words "must believe" (pisteusai dei) mean necessary and essential, absolutely necessary and essential. A.T. Robertson says it is a "moral necessity to have faith. ... The very Existence of God is a matter of intelligent faith ... so that men are left without excuse (Ro. 1:19f)" (*Word Pictures In The New Testament*, Vol. 5, p. 420f).

   - A person must look at the worlds (heaven and earth) and at himself—at the existence, design, order, and end of all things—and believe in God.
   - A person must look at the Word of God, the Holy Bible, and believe in God.
   - A person must look at Jesus Christ, the very Son of God, who reveals God to man, and believe in God.

   b. He must believe that God rewards those who earnestly seek Him. Note the word "earnestly" (ekzetousin). It means to seek out God; to sincerely seek to find Him and to follow Him. God does not reward the sleepy-eyed, complacent, non-thinker, half-interested, worldly-minded, pleasure seeker. God rewards those who earnestly seek to know and follow Him. The idea is that we must be in earnest and persevere and endure to the end. What is the reward to those who earnestly seek God? It is the same reward given to Abel and Enoch: righteousness and God's care in this life and deliverance from death unto eternal life.

> **"So I say to you: Ask and it will be given to you; seek and you will find; knock and the door will be opened to you. For everyone who asks receives; he who seeks finds; and to him who knocks, the door will be opened. (Luke 11:9-10)**
> **Then they asked him, "What must we do to do the works God requires?" Jesus answered, "The work of God is this: to believe in the one he has sent." (John 6:28-29)**
> **God did this so that men would seek him and perhaps reach out for him and find him, though he is not far from each one of us. (Acts 17:27)**
> **Consequently, faith comes from hearing the message, and the message is heard through the word of Christ. (Rom. 10:17)**
> **And this is his command: to believe in the name of his Son, Jesus Christ, and to love one another as he commanded us. (1 John 3:23)**
> **But if from there you seek the LORD your God, you will find him if you look for him with all your heart and with all your soul. (Deut. 4:29)**
> **If my people, who are called by my name, will humble themselves and pray and seek my face and turn from their wicked ways, then will I hear from heaven and will forgive their sin and will heal their land. (2 Chr. 7:14)**
> **I love those who love me, and those who seek me find me. (Prov. 8:17)**
> **You will seek me and find me when you seek me with all your heart. (Jer. 29:13)**

DEEPER STUDY # 1

(11:6) **Faith:** a person can grow in faith and power. Faith and power can be developed by doing two things.

1. By practicing hope (Heb. 11:1), that is, by hoping for something and claiming it because God has promised it.

2. By earnestly seeking God (Heb. 11:6). Christ tells us what is meant by earnest seeking. It means …

    a. To "hunger and thirst after righteousness" (Mt. 5:6).

    b. To "ask … seek … knock" (Mt. 7:7–8).

    c. To "seek first His kingdom and His righteousness" (Mt. 6:33).

The person who needs something and lives on his face in prayer before God (asking, seeking, and knocking) will experience God answering his need. Thus he will be encouraged to trust God, that is, to seek and knock even more and more. A genuine *faith in God* lives before God. That is what faith is: living before God. Faith is entrusting one's life to God. It is trusting God, depending upon God, believing God, seeking God, conversing with God, sharing with God, and fellowshiping with God. A person who really believes that God exists will do these things.

The greater the need, the greater amount of time *true faith* spends alone with God discussing the need. The greater the need, the more earnest *true faith* seeks the answer to its need.

What happens is this: as a person *earnestly* seeks God, he discovers that *true faith* diligently lives before God in prayer and devotion and is given what it hopes for. Therefore the person learns to trust God more and more. He grows in faith.

One thing, however, always needs to be remembered. God is not going to reward sinful, carnal trust, nor is He going to reward a doubting trust. If He answered a doubting trust or a carnal hope and prayer, then the doubting and carnal person would begin to think that the life he is living is acceptable to God. God does not approve sinful and carnal living, nor does He approve a doubting heart. God honors righteous living and a believing heart. It is the person who truly lives righteously and believes enough to earnestly seek God who grows and grows in faith (Jas. 4:3; 1 Cor. 3:1–3. Cp. Mt. 20:21.)

	E. Noah's Faith: A Fearful, Reverent Faith,[DS1] **11:7**

1 **His faith: A faith that promptly obeyed with fear**
2 **His reward**
  a. His family was saved
  b. The world was condemned
  c. He was counted righteous
	7 By faith Noah, when warned about things not yet seen, in holy fear built an ark to save his family. By his faith he condemned the world and became heir of the righteousness that comes by faith.

DIVISION IV

THE SUPREME AUTHOR OF FAITH: JESUS CHRIST, GOD'S SON, 10:19–11:40

E. Noah's Faith: A Fearful, Reverent Faith, 11:7

(11:7) **Introduction:** Noah stands as a great example in believing God and in believing God's warning of coming judgment. His faith was unique in that it was a fearful, reverent faith.

  1. His faith: a faith that promptly obeyed with fear (v. 7).
  2. His reward (v. 7).

DEEPER STUDY # 1

(11:7–40) **Faith:** this begins the list of the believers included in God's Great Hall of Fame. The first two mentioned, Abel and Enoch, should also be added to it, although they are discussed in the overall description of faith. They illustrate the spiritual power of faith (v. 4–5).

Note: each of the believers illustrate a certain kind of faith. For example, glance at the title of Noah's faith above and it is seen that he illustrates a fearful, reverent faith. A glance at the Outline of Hebrews, pt. IV, will give the reader a quick overview of the various kinds of faith illustrated by the great men and women of God. They stand as dynamic examples to us, a stirring challenge for us to believe God in the midst of a corrupt, godless, and dying world.

Note that many of these are covered in one verse or just a few verses at most. However, they are separated and discussed in separate outlines in order to stress their unique faith. The preacher and teacher may wish to cover several in one message or lesson.

---

1 (11:7) **Noah—Faith:** Noah's faith was a faith that promptly obeyed with fear (cp. Gen. 5:5–8:22).

> **By faith Noah, when warned about things not yet seen, in holy fear built an ark to save his family. By his faith he condemned the world and became heir of the righteousness that comes by faith. (Heb. 11:7)**
> **The LORD saw how great man's wickedness on the earth had become, and that every inclination of the thoughts of his heart was only evil all the time. The LORD was grieved that he had made man on the earth, and his**

> **heart was filled with pain. So the LORD said, "I will wipe mankind, whom I have created, from the face of the earth—men and animals, and creatures that move along the ground, and birds of the air—for I am grieved that I have made them." But Noah found favor in the eyes of the LORD. Now the earth was corrupt in God's sight and was full of violence. God saw how corrupt the earth had become, for all the people on earth had corrupted their ways. So God said to Noah, "I am going to put an end to all people, for the earth is filled with violence because of them. I am surely going to destroy both them and the earth. So make yourself an ark of cypress wood; make rooms in it and coat it with pitch inside and out. I am going to bring floodwaters on the earth to destroy all life under the heavens, every creature that has the breath of life in it. Everything on earth will perish. But I will establish my covenant with you, and you will enter the ark—you and your sons and your wife and your sons' wives with you. You are to bring into the ark two of all living creatures, male and female, to keep them alive with you. Noah did everything just as God commanded him. (Gen. 6:5–8, 11–14, 17–19, 22)**

Note two points about Noah's faith.

1. There was a time back in world history when the earth had become so wicked that it was filled with corruption and violence. It was so corrupt that every imagination of man's heart was corrupt and evil. Man had reached the point of no return; he would never repent and return to God. God was left with no choice: the earth had to be destroyed. But there was one man on earth who was godly—Noah. Noah worshipped and honored God in his life. Therefore, God warned Noah of the coming judgment upon the earth.

    ☞ God told Noah to prepare an ark and the ark would save him, his family, and two of every animal.
    ☞ God also told Noah to warn the world of coming judgment.

Note how Noah received the warning from God: he was "in holy fear." The word "fear" (eulabethe) means with godly fear (A. T. Robertson *Word Pictures In The New Testament*, Vol. 5, p. 421). It has the idea of ...

- reverence
- standing in awe of God and His warning
- taking heed lest one fall under God's judgment
- diligently taking God at His Word
- immediately acting upon what God says

Noah believed God's warning of coming judgment, and he began to build the ark with a godly fear and reverence, knowing that what God said would come true. God's judgment would fall upon the earth; Noah believed it and knew it by faith.

Thought 1. God is going to judge the earth a second time—the whole earth, every man and woman. God has warned the earth. His judgment upon the corruption and violence of men is going to fall upon men. We must fear God, fear Him...

- with a godly fear and reverence.
- by standing in awe of Him and His warning.
- by taking heed lest we fall under His judgment.
- by diligently taking Him at His Word.
- by immediately acting upon what He has said.

Our only hope is to believe God, believe Him with a fearful, reverent faith.

2. Noah stood fast in his faith despite the mockery of the world. Noah lived far, far inland from the ocean; he was nowhere close to the sea or to the shipbuilding yards of the world. Yet, there he was building a ship as large as an ocean liner. Imagine the laughs, mockery, scorn, and abuse Noah suffered. Imagine how often he was called a fool and thought to be insane. But Noah was faithful:

- ✏ He preached the righteousness and coming judgment of God. In the eyes of the world he was nothing more than a *fool preacher*, but the mockery and abuse did not deter him. He remained faithful and continued to proclaim the truth and to warn the people—all just like God had told him to do.
- ✏ He also continued to build the ark—continued to work at saving himself and his own house and as much life as possible upon earth. Noah continued on and on, walking in godly fear, believing the sheer Word of God about coming judgment.

Thought 1. A world that lives by science and technology is tempted to trust in nothing beyond itself. Science and technology tend to draw and focus all attention upon the world of sense and feelings, of comfort, and pleasure, of possessions and self. Therefore, the idea of God and of coming judgment is ignored. And if anyone preaches it, he is ridiculed, mocked, scorned, and often abused. We must be faithful to God, for God *exists*. God does exist, and God is going to judge the world.

> "When the Son of Man comes in his glory, and all the angels with him, he will sit on his throne in heavenly glory. All the nations will be gathered before him, and he will separate the

people one from another as a shepherd separates the sheep from the goats. (Matt. 25:31-32)

Just as man is destined to die once, and after that to face judgment, (Heb. 9:27)

If this is so, then the Lord knows how to rescue godly men from trials and to hold the unrighteous for the day of judgment, while continuing their punishment. (2 Pet. 2:9)

By the same word the present heavens and earth are reserved for fire, being kept for the day of judgment and destruction of ungodly men. (2 Pet. 3:7)

In this way, love is made complete among us so that we will have confidence on the day of judgment, because in this world we are like him. (1 John 4:17)

Enoch, the seventh from Adam, prophesied about these men: "See, the Lord is coming with thousands upon thousands of his holy ones to judge everyone, and to convict all the ungodly of all the ungodly acts they have done in the ungodly way, and of all the harsh words ungodly sinners have spoken against him." (Jude 1:14–15)

Moreover, the Father judges no one, but has entrusted all judgment to the Son, (John 5:22)

He commanded us to preach to the people and to testify that he is the one whom God appointed as judge of the living and the dead. (Acts 10:42)

For he has set a day when he will judge the world with justice by the man he has appointed. He has given proof of this to all men by raising him from the dead." (Acts 17:31)

This will take place on the day when God will judge men's secrets through Jesus Christ, as my gospel declares. (Rom. 2:16)

You, then, why do you judge your brother? Or why do you look down on your brother? For we will all stand before God's judgment seat. (Rom. 14:10)

In the presence of God and of Christ Jesus, who will judge the living and the dead, and in view of his appearing and his kingdom, I give you this charge: (2 Tim. 4:1)

And give relief to you who are troubled, and to us as well. This will happen when the Lord Jesus is revealed from heaven in blazing fire with his powerful angels. He will punish those who do not know God and do not obey the gospel of our Lord Jesus. (2 Thes. 1:7-8)

They will sing before the LORD, for he comes, he comes to judge the earth. He will judge the world in righteousness and the peoples in his truth. (Psa. 96:13)

I thought in my heart, "God will bring to judgment both the righteous and the wicked, for there will be a time for every activity, a time for every deed." (Eccl. 3:17)

2 (11:7) **Noah—Faith:** Noah's reward was threefold.

1. Noah's family was saved. Noah believed God—believed the warning of God about coming judgment. Therefore, God saved him. Everyone else around Noah died—to be separated

from God forever. Why? Because they did not believe God's warning about coming judgment. Note that Noah's whole family was saved. Noah's wife and children were blessed to have a godly father, a father who could teach and guide them into the truth. Remember that his sons had married. The young ladies who had married them had done so despite the stigma of the family being a God-fearing family. They could have married men of the world, but they chose to join the family of God, identifying themselves with the God of God's people. Therefore, God saved them as well as Noah (Matthew Henry. *Matthew Henry's Commentary,* Vol. 6, p. 941).

2. The world was condemned; that is, Noah's faith was vindicated. The world had mocked and ridiculed Noah's faith and belief in God's warning of judgment. But God vindicated Noah's faith; God judged the world. And the world saw that Noah had been right all the time.

William Barclay states it well:

> "Noah's faith was a judgment on others. That is why, at least in one sense, it is dangerous to be a Christian. It is not that the Christian is self-righteous; it is not that the Christian is censorious; it is not that the Christian goes about finding fault with other people; it is not that the Christian says: 'I told you so.' It often happens that the Christian simply by being himself is passing judgment on other people. Alcibiades that brilliant, but wild, young man of Athens used to say to Socrates: 'Socrates, I hate you, for every time I meet you, you show me what I am.' One of the finest men who ever lived in Athens was Aristides, who was called 'the just.' But they voted to banish and to ostracise him. One man, being asked why he had so voted, answered: 'Because I am tired of hearing Aristides called the just. There is a danger in goodness, for in the light of goodness evil stands condemned" (The Letter to the Hebrews, p. 160).

3. Noah was counted righteous (dikaios). Noah believed God and God counted his faith as righteousness. He "became heir of the righteousness *that comes by faith.*" As Matthew Henry says, Noah had faith in the *promised Seed,* the Savior whom God was someday going to send to earth (*Matthew Henry's Commentary*, Vol. 6, p. 941). There is nothing else upon earth that can cause God to count a man righteous but faith—faith in the promised Seed, the Savior of the world, even the Lord Jesus Christ.

> **Abram believed the LORD, and he credited it to him as righteousness. (Gen. 15:6)**
>
> **Through him everyone who believes is justified from everything you could not be justified from by the law of Moses. (Acts 13:39)**
>
> **For all have sinned and fall short of the glory of God, and are justified freely by his grace through the redemption that came by Christ Jesus. (Rom. 3:23–24)**
>
> **What does the Scripture say? "Abraham believed God, and it was credited to him as righteousness." (Rom. 4:3)**
>
> **Therefore, since we have been justified through faith, we have peace with God through our Lord Jesus Christ, (Rom. 5:1)**
>
> **Since we have now been justified by his blood, how much more shall we be saved from God's wrath through him! (Rom. 5:9)**
>
> **Because anyone who has died has been freed from sin. (Rom. 6:7)**
>
> **Who will bring any charge against those whom God has chosen? It is God who justifies. (Rom. 8:33)**
>
> **And that is what some of you were. But you were washed, you were sanctified, you were justified in the name of the Lord Jesus Christ and by the Spirit of our God. (1 Cor. 6:11)**
>
> **Know that a man is not justified by observing the law, but by faith in Jesus Christ. So we, too, have put our faith in Christ Jesus that we may be justified by faith in Christ and not by observing the law, because by observing the law no one will be justified. (Gal. 2:16)**
>
> **Consider Abraham: "He believed God, and it was credited to him as righteousness." (Gal. 3:6)**
>
> **So the law was put in charge to lead us to Christ that we might be justified by faith. (Gal. 3:24)**
>
> **And be found in him, not having a righteousness of my own that comes from the law, but that which is through faith in Christ—the righteousness that comes from God and is by faith. (Phil. 3:9)**

	F. Abraham's Faith (Part I): An Obedient, Hopeful Faith, 11:8–10
1 His faith: A faith that obeyed God^DS1 　a. The great call of Abraham 　b. The great faith of Abraham 　　1) A decisive, obedient faith: Obeyed God's call 　　2) A hopeful, obedient faith: Continued to follow God—as a pilgrim **2 His reward: The hope that looked for a heavenly city**	8 By faith Abraham, when called to go to a place he would later receive as his inheritance, obeyed and went, even though he did not know where he was going. 9 By faith he made his home in the promised land like a stranger in a foreign country; he lived in tents, as did Isaac and Jacob, who were heirs with him of the same promise. 10 For he was looking forward to the city with foundations, whose architect and builder is God.

DIVISION IV

THE SUPREME AUTHOR OF FAITH: JESUS CHRIST, GOD'S SON, 10:19–11:40

F. Abraham's Faith (Part I): An Obedient, Hopeful Faith, 11:8–10

(11:8–10) **Introduction:** Abraham demonstrates one of the greatest examples of faith in the Bible. He believed against all odds and he endured in his faith. Abraham's faith was an obedient, believing faith—a faith that genuinely obeyed and believed God.

　1. His faith: a faith that obeyed God (v. 8–9).
　2. His reward: the hope that looked for a heavenly city (v. 10).

1 (11:8–9) **Abraham—Faith:** Abraham's faith was a faith that obeyed and hoped in God. (See Deeper Study # 1—Jn. 4:22; notes—Ro. 4:1–25; 9:7–13; Gal. 3:6–7; 3:8–9; Deeper Study # 1—3:8, 16.)

> The LORD had said to Abram, "Leave your country, your people and your father's household and go to the land I will show you. "I will make you into a great nation and I will bless you; I will make your name great, and you will be a blessing. I will bless those who bless you, and whoever curses you I will curse; and all peoples on earth will be blessed through you." So Abram left, as the LORD had told him; and Lot went with him. Abram was seventy-five years old when he set out from Haran. He took his wife Sarai, his nephew Lot, all the possessions they had accumulated and the people they had acquired in Haran, and they set out for the land of Canaan, and they arrived there. (Gen. 12:1–5; cp. Gen. 11:26–32)
> The LORD said to Abram after Lot had parted from him, "Lift up your eyes from where you are and look north and south, east and west. All the land that you see I will give to you and your offspring forever. I will make your offspring like the dust of the earth, so that if anyone could count the dust, then your offspring could be counted. Go, walk through the length and breadth of the land, for I am giving it to you." (Gen. 13:14–17)
> After this, the word of the LORD came to Abram in a vision: "Do not be afraid, Abram. I am your shield, your very great reward." But Abram said, "O Sovereign LORD, what can you give me since I remain childless and the one who will inherit my estate is Eliezer of Damascus?" And Abram said, "You have given me no children; so a servant in my household will be my heir." Then the word of the LORD came to him: "This man will not be your heir, but a son coming from your own body will be your heir." He took him outside and said, "Look up at the heavens and count the stars—if indeed you can count them." Then he said to him, "So shall your offspring be." Abram believed the LORD, and he credited it to him as righteousness. He also said to him, "I am the LORD, who brought you out of Ur of the Chaldeans to give you this land to take possession of it." (Gen. 15:1–7)
> When Abram was ninety-nine years old, the LORD appeared to him and said, "I am God Almighty ; walk before me and be blameless. I will confirm my covenant between me and you and will greatly increase your numbers." Abram fell facedown, and God said to him, "As for me, this is my covenant with you: You will be the father of many nations. No longer

will you be called Abram; your name will be Abraham, for I have made you a father of many nations. I will make you very fruitful; I will make nations of you, and kings will come from you. I will establish my covenant as an everlasting covenant between me and you and your descendants after you for the generations to come, to be your God and the God of your descendants after you. (Gen. 17:1–7)

God also said to Abraham, "As for Sarai your wife, you are no longer to call her Sarai; her name will be Sarah. I will bless her and will surely give you a son by her. I will bless her so that she will be the mother of nations; kings of peoples will come from her." Abraham fell facedown; he laughed and said to himself, "Will a son be born to a man a hundred years old? Will Sarah bear a child at the age of ninety?" And Abraham said to God, "If only Ishmael might live under your blessing!" Then God said, "Yes, but your wife Sarah will bear you a son, and you will call him Isaac. I will establish my covenant with him as an everlasting covenant for his descendants after him. (Gen. 17:15–19)

The angel of the LORD called to Abraham from heaven a second time and said, "I swear by myself, declares the LORD, that because you have done this and have not withheld your son, your only son, I will surely bless you and make your descendants as numerous as the stars in the sky and as the sand on the seashore. Your descendants will take possession of the cities of their enemies, and through your offspring all nations on earth will be blessed, because you have obeyed me." (Gen. 22:15–18)

To this he replied: "Brothers and fathers, listen to me! The God of glory appeared to our father Abraham while he was still in Mesopotamia, before he lived in Haran. 'Leave your country and your people,' God said, 'and go to the land I will show you.' (Acts 7:2–3)

By faith Abraham, when called to go to a place he would later receive as his inheritance, obeyed and went, even though he did not know where he was going. By faith he made his home in the promised land like a stranger in a foreign country; he lived in tents, as did Isaac and Jacob, who were heirs with him of the same promise. For he was looking forward to the city with foundations, whose architect and builder is God. (Heb. 11:8–10)

Note two things about Abraham's faith.

1. God gave Abraham a great call. He called and challenged Abraham to be a witness to the other people of the world—a witness to the only living and true God. God challenged Abraham to separate himself from the world and to follow God—to leave his home, friends, employment, and his country. If Abraham would heed and obey God's call—if Abraham would obey God unquestionably—then God would do three wonderful things for Abraham.

- God would cause a people to be born of his seed (Gen. 12:1–5; Ro. 4:17–18).

- God would bless all nations through his seed (Gen. 12:2; Ro. 4:17–18; Gal. 3:8, 16).

- God would give him a promised land, the land of Canaan (Gen. 12:1; Ro. 4:13; Heb. 11:8–10, 13–16).

Because those who are led by the Spirit of God are sons of God. For you did not receive a spirit that makes you a slave again to fear, but you received the Spirit of sonship. And by him we cry, "Abba, Father." The Spirit himself testifies with our spirit that we are God's children. Now if we are children, then we are heirs—heirs of God and co-heirs with Christ, if indeed we share in his sufferings in order that we may also share in his glory. (Rom. 8:14–17)

"Therefore come out from them and be separate, says the Lord. Touch no unclean thing, and I will receive you." "I will be a Father to you, and you will be my sons and daughters, says the Lord Almighty." (2 Cor. 6:17–18)

Who wants all men to be saved and to come to a knowledge of the truth. (1 Tim. 2:4)

2. Abraham obeyed God; he believed God. Note exactly the kind of faith he had.

a. He had a *decisive, obedient faith*. He obeyed, and he went out not knowing where he was going. When God called, he acted immediately. He did not hesitate, argue, question, equivocate, or waver back and forth. He obeyed. As soon as he heard the call of God, he got up and followed God: he acted decisively.

Note a significant fact about following God. Abraham did not know where he was going. He did not know where following God would lead him. He just believed the promises of God; therefore, he acted upon his belief. He believed; therefore, he obeyed.

Thought 1. A person who truly believes God obeys God. There is no such thing as belief without obedience, not genuine belief.

Thought 2. No person knows where his faith will lead him, but he is not to fear following God. God is good and He has only good things in store for any true follower of His. If we shrink back and do not believe and follow God, then we shall miss out on the promises of God.

b. He had a hopeful, obedient faith. Note that Abraham never received the inheritance of the promised land, and he never saw a nation of people born of his seed. In fact, Abraham never even owned a piece of land upon which he could settle and live. He was only a *stranger*, a wanderer from place to place in a strange country. He even lived to a ripe old age, seeing both his son and grandson born, and he witnessed them become the heirs of promise. But even they were heirs of the promise, not the inheritors of the land. He never even saw them receive one parcel of land. But despite it all—despite what appeared to be all kinds of odds against the promises of God ever being fulfilled—Abraham still believed in God. He still believed in the hope God had given him. He believed it so strongly that he even taught *the same promises* to his son Isaac and to his grandson Jacob.

"Not everyone who says to me, 'Lord, Lord,' will enter the kingdom of heaven, but only he who does the will of my Father who is in heaven. (Matt. 7:21)

"Therefore everyone who hears these words of mine and puts them into practice is like a wise man who built his house on the rock. The rain came down, the streams rose, and the winds blew and beat against that house; yet it did not fall, because it had its foundation on the rock. (Matt. 7:24–25)

And, once made perfect, he became the source of eternal salvation for all who obey him (Heb. 5:9)

"Blessed are those who wash their robes, that they may have the right to the tree of life and may go through the gates into the city. (Rev. 22:14)

DEEPER STUDY # 1

(11:8–9) **Abraham—Faith**: What did Abraham believe? (See DEEPER STUDY # 1—Ro. 4:1–25; note—9:7–13; DEEPER STUDY # 1—Gal. 3:8, 16.)

1. He believed that God would create a nation through his seed (Gen.12:2-5; Ro.4:17–18).
2. He believed that God would give a child against all odds (Gen. 15:1–6; Ro. 4:18–22; Heb. 11:11–12).
3. He believed in the eternal city (Heb. 11:8–10, 13–16).
4. He believed in God's power to raise the dead (Heb. 11:17–19).

---

2 (11:10) **Abraham—Faith:** Abraham's reward was the great city which had foundations, whose architect and maker is God. The great heavenly city was his hope. This verse plainly says that Abraham's faith was the faith that looked beyond this world to heaven. This is a phenomenal declaration: that Abraham believed in the heavenly city of God, in a future life—a life that would put him in the presence of God forever and ever. Yet, this is exactly what is declared in this Scripture by the Holy Spirit through the writer to the Hebrews. Paul even says that the promise made to Abraham was "that he would be heir of the world" (Ro. 4:13). This refers, of course, to the new heavens and earth (cp. 2 Pt. 3:10–13; Rev. 21:1f).

The point to see is the great faith of Abraham. He believed that God was going to give him the land of Canaan which was a type or symbol of the great land of heaven, the great city whose architect is God.

It was not through law that Abraham and his offspring received the promise that he would be heir of the world, but through the righteousness that comes by faith. (Rom. 4:13)

For he was looking forward to the city with foundations, whose architect and builder is God. (Heb. 11:10)

Instead, they were longing for a better country—a heavenly one. Therefore God is not ashamed to be called their God, for he has prepared a city for them. (Heb. 11:16)

But you have come to Mount Zion, to the heavenly Jerusalem, the city of the living God. You have come to thousands upon thousands of angels in joyful assembly, (Heb. 12:22)

For here we do not have an enduring city, but we are looking for the city that is to come. (Heb. 13:14)

But the day of the Lord will come like a thief. The heavens will disappear with a roar; the elements will be destroyed by fire, and the earth and everything in it will be laid bare. Since everything will be destroyed in this way, what kind of people ought you to be? You ought to live holy and godly lives as you look forward to the day of God and speed its coming. That day will bring about the destruction of the heavens by fire, and the elements will melt in the heat. But in keeping with his promise we are looking forward to a new heaven and a new earth, the home of righteousness. (2 Pet. 3:10–13)

Then I saw a new heaven and a new earth, for the first heaven and the first earth had passed away, and there was no longer any sea. I saw the Holy City, the new Jerusalem, coming down out of heaven from God, prepared as a bride beautifully dressed for her husband. And I heard a loud voice from the throne saying, "Now the dwelling of God is with men, and he will live with them. They will be his people, and God himself will be with them and be their God. He will wipe every tear from their eyes. There will be no more death or mourning or crying or pain, for the old order of things has passed away." (Rev. 21:1–4)

And he carried me away in the Spirit to a mountain great and high, and showed me the Holy City, Jerusalem, coming down out of heaven from God. (Rev. 21:10)

"Blessed are those who wash their robes, that they may have the right to the tree of life and may go through the gates into the city. (Rev. 22:14)

And if anyone takes words away from this book of prophecy, God will take away from him his share in the tree of life and in the holy city, which are described in this book. (Rev. 22:19)

		G. Sarah's Faith: An Impossible Faith, 11:11–12
1	Her faith: A faith that believed the impossible	11 By faith Abraham, even though he was past age—and Sarah herself was barren—was enabled to become a father because he considered him faithful who had made the promise.
2	Her reward: The promised son & nation	12 And so from this one man, and he as good as dead, came descendants as numerous as the stars in the sky and as countless as the sand on the seashore.

DIVISION IV

THE SUPREME AUTHOR OF FAITH: JESUS CHRIST, GOD'S SON, 10:19–11:40

G. Sarah's Faith: An Impossible Faith, 11:11–12

(11:11–12) **Introduction:** Sarah is a dynamic example of what it is to believe the impossible. She believed the impossible; therefore, she saw God do the impossible.

1. Her faith: a faith that believed the impossible (v. 11).
2. Her reward: the promised son and nation (v. 12).

1 (11:11) **Sarah—Faith:** Sarah's faith was a faith that believed the impossible.

"Where is your wife Sarah?" they asked him. "There, in the tent," he said. Then the LORD said, "I will surely return to you about this time next year, and Sarah your wife will have a son." Now Sarah was listening at the entrance to the tent, which was behind him. Abraham and Sarah were already old and well advanced in years, and Sarah was past the age of childbearing. So Sarah laughed to herself as she thought, "After I am worn out and my master is old, will I now have this pleasure?" Then the LORD said to Abraham, "Why did Sarah laugh and say, 'Will I really have a child, now that I am old?' Is anything too hard for the LORD? I will return to you at the appointed time next year and Sarah will have a son." Sarah was afraid, so she lied and said, "I did not laugh." But he said, "Yes, you did laugh." (Gen. 18:9-15; cp. Gen. 17:15–22)
Now the LORD was gracious to Sarah as he had said, and the LORD did for Sarah what he had promised. Sarah became pregnant and bore a son to Abraham in his old age, at the very time God had promised him. Abraham gave the name Isaac to the son Sarah bore him. When his son Isaac was eight days old, Abraham circumcised him, as God command-

ed him. Abraham was a hundred years old when his son Isaac was born to him. (Gen. 21:1–5)
Against all hope, Abraham in hope believed and so became the father of many nations, just as it had been said to him, "So shall your offspring be." Without weakning in his faith, he faced the fact that his body was as good as dead—since he was about a hundred years old—and that Sarah's womb was also dead. Yet he did not waver through unbelief regarding the promise of God, but was strengthened in his faith and gave glory to God, being fully persuaded that God had power to do what he had promised. (Rom. 4:18–21)
By faith Abraham, even though he was past age—and Sarah herself was barren [90 years old]—was enabled to become a father because he considered him faithful who had made the promise. And so from this one man, and he as good as dead, came descendants as numerous as the stars in the sky and as countless as the sand on the seashore. (Heb. 11:11–12)

Note two significant facts.
1. Sarah had difficulty believing God at first. When she first heard the promise of God she doubted the promise. In the Genesis account the Lord appeared and talked with Abraham right outside the door of Abraham's tent. Sarah hid in the tent with her ear up close so she could hear the conversation. When she overheard the Lord promise a child to Abraham, Sarah laughed, for she and Abraham were well past child-bearing age (cp. Gen. 18:12). They were both humanly sterile.

Thought 1. The promises of God do sound unbelievable. Just think how corrupt, sinful, evil, savage, violent, and doomed to death the human race is. Any daily news media is filled with illustrations of man's corruption. Yet God loves the world, loves it so much that He has promised "the seed" of the Savior to the world. Just think how unbelievable this sounds.

- ✎ God has promised a Savior who will bear the sins of man for him and present him to God as righteous.
- ✎ God has promised a Savior who will save man from the corruption and death of the world, a Savior who can give man life—eternal life in a new heavens and earth.

2. Sarah considered the matter: who it was that was making the promise, God Himself, the Sovereign Majesty of the universe. When Sarah considered this, the change in her was dramatic: if it was God who was making the promise, then God could be *counted (judged)* faithful. God always fulfills His promises. God could do it no matter how difficult the situation was …

- despite the human impossibility.
- despite the fact that all reason spoke against it.
- despite the fact that nature had to be overridden.

Sarah believed God. She switched from unbelief to belief. She trusted the promise of God. Therefore, she bore a child at the age of ninety. It was a miraculous birth, but God had promised and He fulfilled His promise.

Thought 1. God cannot lie; He cannot deceive people. Therefore, the promises of God—every single one of them—shall be fulfilled. But note: the promise of the *seed*, that is, of the Savior, applies only to those who believe.

> Jesus looked at them and said, "With man this is impossible, but with God all things are possible." (Matt. 19:26)
>
> "'If you can'?" said Jesus. "Everything is possible for him who believes." (Mark 9:23)
>
> "Abba, Father," he said, "everything is possible for you. Take this cup from me. Yet not what I will, but what you will." (Mark 14:36)
>
> For nothing is impossible with God." (Luke 1:37)
>
> "I know that you can do all things; no plan of yours can be thwarted. (Job 42:2)
>
> How great is your goodness, which you have stored up for those who fear you, which you bestow in the sight of men on those who take refuge in you. (Psa. 31:19)
>
> Commit your way to the LORD; trust in him and he will do this: (Psa. 37:5)
>
> One thing God has spoken, two things have I heard: that you, O God, are strong, (Psa. 62:11)
>
> Trust in the LORD with all your heart and lean not on your own understanding; (Prov. 3:5)

> Trust in the LORD forever, for the LORD, the LORD, is the Rock eternal. (Isa. 26:4)

2 (11:12) **Sarah—Faith:** Sarah's faith was rewarded. She received the promised son and nation through her seed. This refers to two rewards:

- ✎ the gift of *the seed Isaac* and of the nation of Israel.
- ✎ the gift of *the seed Christ* and of the nation of believers, of the new creation of born again men and women, those who shall be citizens of God's new heavens and earth (see DEEPER STUDY # 1—Gal. 3:8, notes—Gal. 3:16; Eph. 2:11–18; 2:14–15; 3:16; 4:17–19. See DEEPER STUDY # 1—Jn. 4:22; DEEPER STUDY # 1—Ro. 4:1–25.)

Sarah believed the impossible, and God rewarded her faith: she *received* the impossible. Look at Israel. Israel exists today because Sarah believed the impossible promise of God. Look at the believers around the world, those who profess to be born again by the sacrifice of Jesus Christ for their sins. They exist today because Sarah believed the impossible promise of God.

> In reply Jesus declared, "I tell you the truth, no one can see the kingdom of God unless he is born again." Jesus answered, "I tell you the truth, no one can enter the kingdom of God unless he is born of water and the Spirit. Flesh gives birth to flesh, but the Spirit gives birth to spirit. You should not be surprised at my saying, 'You must be born again.' (John 3:3, 5–7)
>
> Therefore, if anyone is in Christ, he is a new creation; the old has gone, the new has come! (2 Cor. 5:17)
>
> For you have been born again, not of perishable seed, but of imperishable, through the living and enduring word of God. (1 Pet. 1:23)
>
> Everyone who believes that Jesus is the Christ is born of God, and everyone who loves the father loves his child as well. (1 John 5:1)
>
> And without faith it is impossible to please God, because anyone who comes to him must believe that he exists and that he rewards those who earnestly seek him. (Heb. 11:6)
>
> A man is not a Jew if he is only one outwardly, nor is circumcision merely outward and physical. No, a man is a Jew if he is one inwardly; and circumcision is circumcision of the heart, by the Spirit, not by the written code. Such a man's praise is not from men, but from God. (Rom. 2:28–29)
>
> If you belong to Christ, then you are Abraham's seed, and heirs according to the promise. (Gal. 3:29)

	H. The Patriarch's Faith: A Pilgrim's Faith, 11:13–16	14 People who say such things show that they are looking for a country of their own. 15 If they had been thinking of the country they had left, they would have had opportunity to return. 16 Instead, they were longing for a better country—a heavenly one. Therefore God is not ashamed to be called their God, for he has prepared a city for them.	c. A working faith: They sought & declared that they were seeking a country of their own d. An enduring faith: They did not return
1 Their faith: A faith that endures—that forever seeks an unseen, heavenly country a. A visionary faith: They saw b. A growing faith: They saw, and welcomed the promises of God	13 All these people were still living by faith when they died. They did not receive the things promised; they only saw them and welcomed them from a distance. And they admitted that they were aliens and strangers on earth.		2 Their reward a. God's approval b. God's prepared city

DIVISION IV

THE SUPREME AUTHOR OF FAITH: JESUS CHRIST, GOD'S SON, 10:19–11:40

H. The Patriarch's Faith: A Pilgrim's Faith, 11:13–16

(11:13–16) **Introduction:** believers are only strangers and pilgrims on earth. They are only passing through this earth and this life which is ever so brief and corrupt. They are heirs and citizens of heaven. This passage is a picture of the great faith of believers, the faith of God's pilgrims upon earth.

1. Their faith: a faith that endures that forever seeks an unseen, heavenly country (v. 13–15).
2. Their reward (v. 16).

1 (11:13–15) **Patriarchs—Faith—Pilgrimage:** the patriarch's faith was a faith that endured, that forever sought an unseen, heavenly country. The word patriarch refers to Abraham, Isaac, Jacob, and other ancient men who had great faith in God and His promises. The point to see is this: these all died believing what God had promised and not a single one of them ever received the promise on earth. If they were to receive them, they had to accept them by faith. Believing them—hoping in them—was the only way they could possess them. Note four points.

1. Their faith was a *visionary faith*. They saw the promises of God afar off, not by sight but in their hearts and minds. What was the promise? It was the promise …
   • of a country (v. 14).
   • of a better country, a heavenly world (v. 16). Christ Jesus even said that Abraham saw His day and rejoiced in the hope of it (cp. Jn. 8:56).

Thought 1. How much more we can see and understand the promises of God. Christ has already come once. To believe that He shall return is much easier than Abraham believing that He was coming the first time. Abraham had no precedent, whereas we do.

2. Their faith was a *growing faith*.
   ➯ They saw the promise of God and were thankful to God for the privilege of seeing it.

   ➯ They were persuaded of the promises of God. They believed that the promises were true, that there was a promised land and that God was going to give it to them. They believed in God and that what God promised He was going to fulfill.
   ➯ They welcomed (aspasamenoi) the promises. The word means to greet and welcome. They were ever so thankful and appreciative to God for such a glorious hope as the promised land. They rejoiced and loved the promise, setting their eyes upon it and not looking away.
   ➯ They admitted that they were only aliens and strangers on earth, just passing through until they could inherit the glorious hope of the promised land. They confessed the glorious hope to all; they bore testimony and witness and did so unashamedly that God had given them the hope of the promised land.

3. Their faith was a *working faith*. They actively sought after the promised land and declared the fact to all.
   ➯ They did not just sit back and talk about the promised land, thinking that God would take them to it when it was time.
   ➯ They did no go on about their lives upon this earth ignoring the promised land, thinking that they were good enough and God would never reject them from inheriting it.

The early believers actively sought after the promised land. They got up and went looking for it, leaving the world and its possessions behind. By their separation from the world and seeking after God's promises, they showed that they were men and women of true faith.

4. Their faith was an *enduring faith*. They never returned to the country they had left. They had separated from the world and began a search for the promised land of God and they stayed on the search.

Simply stated, they kept their mind and thoughts upon the promised land.

✏ They did not harbor the thoughts of the old world's pleasures and desires, possessions and indulgences, feelings and comforts.

✏ They did not return to the old world when they had the chance.

✏ The patriarchs endured to the end. In fact, they went to their grave believing in the great hope of God for the promised land.

> **Being fully persuaded that God had power to do what he had promised. (Rom. 4:21)**
>
> **For I am convinced that neither death nor life, neither angels nor demons, neither the present nor the future, nor any powers, neither height nor depth, nor anything else in all creation, will be able to separate us from the love of God that is in Christ Jesus our Lord. (Rom. 8:38–39)**
>
> **That is why I am suffering as I am. Yet I am not ashamed, because I know whom I have believed, and am convinced that he is able to guard what I have entrusted to him for that day. (2 Tim. 1:12)**
>
> **But our citizenship is in heaven. And we eagerly await a Savior from there, the Lord Jesus Christ, who, by the power that enables him to bring everything under his control, will transform our lowly bodies so that they will be like his glorious body. (Phil. 3:20–21)**
>
> **All these people were still living by faith when they died. They did not receive the things promised; they only saw them and welcomed them from a distance. And they admitted that they were aliens and strangers on earth. (Heb. 11:13)**
>
> **For here we do not have an enduring city, but we are looking for the city that is to come. (Heb. 13:14)**
>
> **We are aliens and strangers in your sight, as were all our forefathers. Our days on earth are like a shadow, without hope. (1 Chr. 29:15)**
>
> **"Hear my prayer, O LORD, listen to my cry for help; be not deaf to my weeping. For I dwell with you as an alien, a stranger, as all my fathers were. (Psa. 39:12)**
>
> **I am a stranger on earth; do not hide your commands from me. (Psa. 119:19)**

2 (11:16) **Faith—Reward:** the reward of the patriarchs. Their reward was twofold.

1. They received God's approval. God is not ashamed to be called their God. Note the present tense: they are still living, even today. And so is God. God is acting now; it is today that He is unashamed. He is the God of Abraham, Isaac, and Jacob today, and He is not ashamed to be called their God. Just imagine! These great patriarchs have been alive and living in God's presence for thousands of years (cp. Mt. 22:32; Mk. 12:26; Lk. 20:37). God loves and commits Himself to all who believe Him and His promises. He is not ashamed and never will be ashamed of those who confess that they seek Him and the country He has promised.

> **"For God so loved the world that he gave**

> **his one and only Son, that whoever believes in him shall not perish but have eternal life. (John 3:16)**
>
> **If we live, we live to the Lord; and if we die, we die to the Lord. So, whether we live or die, we belong to the Lord. (Rom. 14:8)**
>
> **For to me, to live is Christ and to die is gain. (Phil. 1:21)**
>
> **All these people were still living by faith when they died. They did not receive the things promised; they only saw them and welcomed them from a distance. And they admitted that they were aliens and strangers on earth. (Heb. 11:13)**
>
> **Then I heard a voice from heaven say, "Write: Blessed are the dead who die in the Lord from now on." "Yes," says the Spirit, "they will rest from their labor, for their deeds will follow them." (Rev. 14:13)**
>
> **But accepts men from every nation who fear him and do what is right. (Acts 10:35)**
>
> **Therefore we are always confident and know that as long as we are at home in the body we are away from the Lord. We live by faith, not by sight. We are confident, I say, and would prefer to be away from the body and at home with the Lord. So we make it our goal to please him, whether we are at home in the body or away from it. For we must all appear before the judgment seat of Christ, that each one may receive what is due him for the things done while in the body, whether good or bad. (2 Cor. 5:6–10)**
>
> **"Therefore come out from them and be separate, says the Lord. Touch no unclean thing, and I will receive you." "I will be a Father to you, and you will be my sons and daughters, says the Lord Almighty." (2 Cor. 6:17–18)**
>
> **To the praise of his glorious grace, which he has freely given us in the One he loves. In him we have redemption through his blood, the forgiveness of sins, in accordance with the riches of God's grace (Eph. 1:6–7)**
>
> **Now if you obey me fully and keep my covenant, then out of all nations you will be my treasured possession. Although the whole earth is mine, (Exo. 19:5)**

2. They received the promised land. God prepared a city for them, a heavenly city that will last forever and ever.

> **It was not through law that Abraham and his offspring received the promise that he would be heir of the world, but through the righteousness that comes by faith. (Rom. 4:13)**
>
> **For he was looking forward to the city with foundations, whose architect and builder is God. (Heb. 11:10)**
>
> **Instead, they were longing for a better country—a heavenly one. Therefore God is not ashamed to be called their God, for he has prepared a city for them. (Heb. 11:16)**
>
> **But you have come to Mount Zion, to**

the heavenly Jerusalem, the city of the living God. You have come to thousands upon thousands of angels in joyful assembly, (Heb. 12:22)

For here we do not have an enduring city, but we are looking for the city that is to come. (Heb. 13:14)

But the day of the Lord will come like a thief. The heavens will disappear with a roar; the elements will be destroyed by fire, and the earth and everything in it will be laid bare. Since everything will be destroyed in this way, what kind of people ought you to be? You ought to live holy and godly lives as you look forward to the day of God and speed its coming. That day will bring about the destruction of the heavens by fire, and the elements will melt in the heat. But in keeping with his promise we are looking forward to a new heaven and a new earth, the home of righteousness. (2 Pet. 3:10–13)

Then I saw a new heaven and a new earth, for the first heaven and the first earth had passed away, and there was no longer any sea. I saw the Holy City, the new Jerusalem, coming down out of heaven from God, prepared as a bride beautifully dressed for her husband. And I heard a loud voice from the throne saying, "Now the dwelling of God is with men, and he will live with them. They will be his people, and God himself will be with them and be their God. He will wipe every tear from their eyes. There will be no more death or mourning or crying or pain, for the old order of things has passed away." (Rev. 21:1–4)

And he carried me away in the Spirit to a mountain great and high, and showed me the Holy City, Jerusalem, coming down out of heaven from God. (Rev. 21:10)

"Blessed are those who wash their robes, that they may have the right to the tree of life and may go through the gates into the city. (Rev. 22:14)

And if anyone takes words away from this book of prophecy, God will take away from him his share in the tree of life and in the holy city, which are described in this book. (Rev. 22:19)

	I. Abraham's Faith (Part II): A Sacrificial Faith, 11:17–19
1 His faith: A faith that obeys God regardless of cost a. God's unbelievable command: Sacrifice Isaac b. Abraham's great faith: Counted God as trustworthy **2 His reward: Deliverance**	17 By faith Abraham, when God tested him, offered Isaac as a sacrifice. He who had received the promises was about to sacrifice his one and only son, 18 Even though God had said to him, "It is through Isaac that your offspring will be reckoned." 19 Abraham reasoned that God could raise the dead, and figuratively speaking, he did receive Isaac back from death.

DIVISION IV

THE SUPREME AUTHOR OF FAITH: JESUS CHRIST, GOD'S SON, 10:19–11:40

I. Abraham's Faith (Part II): A Sacrificial Faith, 11:17–19

(11:17–19) **Introduction:** this act of Abraham is the supreme act of faith. This is the picture of sacrificial faith, the faith which God demands of every man, the faith without which a person shall never inherit the promises of God.

   1. His faith: a faith that obeys God regardless of cost (v. 17–19).
   2. His reward: deliverance (v. 19).

1 (11:17–19) **Abraham—Faith:** Abraham's faith was a faith that obeyed God regardless of cost. This demand made upon Abraham was the supreme act of faith (cp. Gen. 22:1–18).

> Some time later God tested Abraham. He said to him, "Abraham!" "Here I am," he replied. Then God said, "Take your son, your only son, Isaac, whom you love, and go to the region of Moriah. Sacrifice him there as a burnt offering on one of the mountains I will tell you about." Early the next morning Abraham got up and saddled his donkey. He took with him two of his servants and his son Isaac. When he had cut enough wood for the burnt offering, he set out for the place God had told him about. (Gen. 22:1–3)
>
> When they reached the place God had told him about, Abraham built an altar there and arranged the wood on it. He bound his son Isaac and laid him on the altar, on top of the wood. Then he reached out his hand and took the knife to slay his son. But the angel of the LORD called out to him from heaven, "Abraham! Abraham!" "Here I am," he replied. "Do not lay a hand on the boy," he said. "Do not do anything to him. Now I know

> that you fear God, because you have not withheld from me your son, your only son." (Gen 22:9–12)
>
> The angel of the LORD called to Abraham from heaven a second time and said, "I swear by myself, declares the LORD, that because you have done this and have not withheld your son, your only son, I will surely bless you and make your descendants as numerous as the stars in the sky and as the sand on the seashore. Your descendants will take possession of the cities of their enemies, and through your offspring all nations on earth will be blessed, because you have obeyed me." (Gen. 22:15–18)
>
> By faith Abraham, when God tested him, offered Isaac as a sacrifice. He who had received the promises was about to sacrifice his one and only son, even though God had said to him, "It is through Isaac that your offspring will be reckoned." Abraham reasoned that God could raise the dead, and figuratively speaking, he did receive Isaac back from death. (Heb. 11:17–19)

Note two significant points.

1. God's unbelievable command. God commanded Abraham to take Isaac and to offer him up as a sacrifice to Him. To say the least this was a most unusual command, that is, God commanding that a human sacrifice be made to Him. William Barclay has a comment about this fact that states it well:

> *"To some extent this story has fallen into disrepute nowadays. It does not appear in syllabuses of religious education because it is held to teach a view of God that can no longer be accepted. Or, failing that, it is held to teach*

28

that the point of the story is that it was in this way that Abraham learned that God did not desire human sacrifice. There were days when men considered it a sacred duty to offer up their first-born sons to God, before they learned that God would never desire a sacrifice like that. No doubt that is true; but if we want to see this story at its greatest, and if we want to see it as the writer to the Hebrews saw it, we must take it at its face value. It was the response of a man who was asked to offer to God his own son" (The Letter to the Hebrews, p.171).

What was God doing? We can say several things.

a. God was testing the faith of Abraham in the most supreme way possible. We must always remember that God had made the supreme promises to Abraham:

- The supreme promise of the seed of the Savior, of God's very own Son.
- The supreme hope of the promised land and of dwelling in the very presence of God Himself. And the inheritance was to be for eternity.
- The supreme promise of an unlimited nation of people, a people that would endure forever.
- The supreme promise of being a blessing to all the nations of the world, an eternal blessing.

A man who had received the supreme promises of God had to be tested in the most supreme way possible. And, no doubt, in light of what God demanded of Abraham, the most supreme way in Abraham's day and time was to demand that Abraham sacrifice his only son. Remember how difficult this was for Abraham. He loved Isaac dearly, for Isaac was not only his only son, but Abraham's whole life—his past and future were wrapped up in Isaac. Abraham had lived for Isaac, his only son. All the promises of God to him were wrapped up in Isaac. What an unbelievable faith Abraham had!

b. God was using the offering of Isaac as a sacrifice to symbolize the offering up of God's only Son as the sacrifice for man's sins. God was also using Abraham's faith that God could raise up the dead to proclaim that man must believe *that God can raise the dead*. God is going to; therefore, man must believe it in order to be resurrected.

> **The next day John saw Jesus coming toward him and said, "Look, the Lamb of God, who takes away the sin of the world! (John 1:29)**
>
> **Greater love has no one than this, that he lay down his life for his friends. (John 15:13)**
>
> **You see, at just the right time, when we were still powerless, Christ died for the ungodly. (Rom. 5:6)**
>
> **For what I received I passed on to you as of first importance : that Christ died for our sins according to the Scriptures, that he was buried, that he was raised on the third day according to the Scriptures, and that he appeared to Peter, and then to the Twelve. (1 Cor. 15:3–5)**

> **Who gave himself for our sins to rescue us from the present evil age, according to the will of our God and Father, (Gal. 1:4)**
>
> **And live a life of love, just as Christ loved us and gave himself up for us as a fragrant offering and sacrifice to God. (Eph. 5:2)**
>
> **Who gave himself for us to redeem us from all wickedness and to purify for himself a people that are his very own, eager to do what is good. (Titus 2:14)**
>
> **For you know that it was not with perishable things such as silver or gold that you were redeemed from the empty way of life handed down to you from your forefathers, but with the precious blood of Christ, a lamb without blemish or defect. (1 Pet. 1:18–19)**
>
> **This is how we know what love is: Jesus Christ laid down his life for us. And we ought to lay down our lives for our brothers. (1 John 3:16)**
>
> **And from Jesus Christ, who is the faithful witness, the firstborn from the dead, and the ruler of the kings of the earth. To him who loves us and has freed us from our sins by his blood, (Rev. 1:5)**

c. God was also teaching that man must trust God to the ultimate degree. Man must be willing to sacrifice the thing he loves the most and holds dearest to his heart. He must love God supremely, love God and His promises above all else. God will not accept second best and divided loyalty. He demands to be first in the life of every person. A person either puts Him first or else he is unacceptable to God and misses out on the promises of God.

2. Abraham's great faith was the ultimate faith. Abraham considered and thought through the demand of God. He knew God was God; therefore ...

- he knew that God gave no foolish commands.
- he knew that God could stop him anywhere along the road to the mountain where he was to sacrifice Isaac, and if not, then God could raise Isaac from the dead.
- he knew that God never broke His promises and that God could not fulfill His promises without Isaac.

Abraham counted God trustworthy—true and faithful to His promise. Therefore, he stepped out to follow God supremely.

Thought 1. Note how Abraham loved God supremely. Abraham put God above all, even above the person whom he loved the most, his own dear son.

> **Jesus looked at them and said, "With man this is impossible, but with God all things are possible." (Matt. 19:26)**
>
> **"'If you can'?" said Jesus. "Everything is possible for him who believes." (Mark 9:23)**
>
> **For nothing is impossible with God." (Luke 1:37)**
>
> **"I tell you the truth, whoever hears my word and believes him who sent me has eternal life and will not be condemned; he has**

crossed over from death to life. (John 5:24)

Consider Abraham: "He believed God, and it was credited to him as righteousness." (Gal. 3:6)

And without faith it is impossible to please God, because anyone who comes to him must believe that he exists and that he rewards those who earnestly seek him. (Heb. 11:6)

In the same way, faith by itself, if it is not accompanied by action, is dead. (James 2:17)

One thing God has spoken, two things have I heard: that you, O God, are strong, (Psa. 62:11)

Our God is in heaven; he does whatever pleases him. (Psa. 115:3)

2 (11:19) **Abraham—Faith—Reward:** Abraham's reward was deliverance, the deliverance of his son from the dead. The idea is this: Isaac was as good as dead in Abraham's mind. Abraham was totally committed to sacrifice Isaac; he was totally committed to love God and His Word supremely. That was enough for God. God had His answer. Abraham believed God and loved Him above the most dear thing on earth. Therefore, when God stopped the judgment upon Isaac, it was like a resurrection from the dead. The point to us is the three lessons given in the former note:

- ☞ We must trust God supremely, love and trust Him above everyone and all else.
- ☞ We must believe God even when we cannot understand the ways and commands of God.
- ☞ We must trust the sacrifice of God's own dear Son for our sins and trust His resurrection as the assurance of our being resurrected and living forever with God.

That everyone who believes in him may have eternal life. "For God so loved the world that he gave his one and only Son, that whoever believes in him shall not perish but have eternal life. (John 3:15–16)

"I tell you the truth, whoever hears my word and believes him who sent me has eternal life and will not be condemned; he has crossed over from death to life. I tell you the truth, a time is coming and has now come when the dead will hear the voice of the Son

of God and those who hear will live. (John 5:24–25)

For my Father's will is that everyone who looks to the Son and believes in him shall have eternal life, and I will raise him up at the last day." (John 6:40)

I tell you the truth, if anyone keeps my word, he will never see death." (John 8:51)

Jesus said to her, "I am the resurrection and the life. He who believes in me will live, even though he dies; (John 11:25)

For the perishable must clothe itself with the imperishable, and the mortal with immortality. When the perishable has been clothed with the imperishable, and the mortal with immortality, then the saying that is written will come true: "Death has been swallowed up in victory." (1 Cor. 15:53–54)

Now we know that if the earthly tent we live in is destroyed, we have a building from God, an eternal house in heaven, not built by human hands. (2 Cor. 5:1)

For the Lord himself will come down from heaven, with a loud command, with the voice of the archangel and with the trumpet call of God, and the dead in Christ will rise first. After that, we who are still alive and are left will be caught up together with them in the clouds to meet the Lord in the air. And so we will be with the Lord forever. Therefore encourage each other with these words. (1 Thess. 4:16–18)

But it has now been revealed through the appearing of our Savior, Christ Jesus, who has destroyed death and has brought life and immortality to light through the gospel. (2 Tim. 1:10)

But God will redeem my life from the grave; he will surely take me to himself. Selah (Psa. 49:15)

Though you have made me see troubles, many and bitter, you will restore my life again; from the depths of the earth you will again bring me up. (Psa. 71:20)

"I will ransom them from the power of the grave ; I will redeem them from death. Where, O death, are your plagues? Where, O grave, is your destruction? "I will have no compassion, (Hosea 13:14)

	J. Isaac's Faith: A Repentant Faith, 11:20
1. A faith that believed in the future despite sin	20 By faith Isaac blessed Jacob and Esau in regard to their future.

DIVISION IV

THE SUPREME AUTHOR OF FAITH: JESUS CHRIST, GOD'S SON, 10:19–11:40

J. Isaac's Faith: A Repentant Faith, 11:20

(11:20) **Introduction:** Isaac is the prime example of a person who believes the promises of God, but needs to repent before he can receive them. Isaac is an example of the person who believes in the future despite sin.

1 (11:20) **Isaac—Faith:** Isaac's faith was a faith that believed in the future despite sin (Gen. 27:1–40). Isaac believed that God would fulfill His promises through his sons, fulfill His promises despite the selfishness and conniving deception of his sons.

Jacob was the younger son who stuck closer to his mother. He was somewhat of a homebody. Esau was Isaac's older son, a true outdoorsman just like Isaac. Therefore, Isaac preferred Esau. He wanted Esau to receive the greater blessing of God, in particular he wanted Esau to be the seed through whom God would fulfill His promise of a promised land and of a nation of people.

Isaac was aged and blind when he was ready to pass the blessing on to his sons. Now note several facts.

- God had told Isaac and his wife, Rebekah, that Jacob was to be the one who was to receive the blessing; the older son was to serve the younger.

  The LORD said to her, "Two nations are in your womb, and two peoples from within you will be separated; one people will be stronger than the other, and the older will serve the younger." (Gen. 25:23)

- Isaac was reluctant to obey God. In fact, he did not want to obey God; he preferred Esau. When it came time to pass the blessings of God's promise on to his son, Isaac planned to ignore God's will and bless Esau.

  When Isaac was old and his eyes were so weak that he could no longer see, he called for Esau his older son and said to him, "My son." "Here I am," he answered. Isaac said, "I am now an old man and don't know the day of my death. Now then, get your weapons—your quiver and bow—and go out to the open country to hunt some wild game for me. Prepare me the kind of tasty food I like and bring it to me to eat, so that I may give you my blessing before I die." (Gen. 27:1–4)

- Rebekah overheard Isaac's plans to ignore and bypass God's will. Therefore, she plotted with Jacob to deceive Isaac and have him pass the blessing on to Jacob. Remember: Isaac was blind and unable to see; therefore Jacob was able to deceive Isaac and receive the blessing.

  Jacob went close to his father Isaac, who touched him and said, "The voice is the voice of Jacob, but the hands are the hands of Esau." He did not recognize him, for his hands were hairy like those of his brother Esau; so he blessed him. "Are you really my son Esau?" he asked. "I am," he replied. Then he said, "My son, bring me some of your game to eat, so that I may give you my blessing." Jacob brought it to him and he ate; and he brought some wine and he drank. Then his father Isaac said to him, "Come here, my son, and kiss me." So he went to him and kissed him. When Isaac caught the smell of his clothes, he blessed him and said, "Ah, the smell of my son is like the smell of a field that the LORD has blessed. May God give you of heaven's dew and of earth's richness—an abundance of grain and new wine. May nations serve you and peoples bow down to you. Be lord over your brothers, and may the sons of your mother bow down to you. May those who curse you be cursed and those who bless you be blessed." (Gen. 27:22–29)

- Isaac refused to reverse the blessing when the deception was discovered. In the final analysis, he repented. He turned away from his own desires and did God's will.

  Isaac trembled violently and said, "Who was it, then, that hunted game and brought it to me? I ate it just before you came and I blessed him—and indeed he will be blessed!" (Gen. 27:33)

The point is this: Isaac's faith was firm about the future despite sin. At first, Isaac was unwilling to follow God and do as God had said. And his son Jacob set out to secure God's blessing by deception. Jacob was unwilling to wait upon God; he felt that he had to help God out even if it meant lying and deceiving. But in the end, Isaac repented: he believed God and he did God's will. He could have easily reversed his blessing, but he refused. He had reached the point where he knew that God's will had to be done. Therefore, he repented and turned from his own will to the will of God.

Note through all of this the strong faith in *regard to their future*. Isaac believed in the promises of God; he believed in the *promised seed* and the *promised land*. He never saw the promises fulfilled, not during his life upon this earth. He was only a pilgrim and sojourner on earth, never seeing the *promised land*. But he believed and held firm to his belief— so firm that he passed the blessing of God's promises down through his son Jacob. Isaac died, but he died as a man of faith, as a man who repented and did God's will.

Blessed are those who mourn, for they will be comforted. (Matt. 5:4)

I tell you, no! But unless you repent, you too will all perish. (Luke 13:3)

Repent, then, and turn to God, so that your sins may be wiped out, that times of refreshing may come from the Lord, (Acts 3:19)

Repent of this wickedness and pray to the Lord. Perhaps he will forgive you for having such a thought in your heart. (Acts 8:22)

In the past God overlooked such ignorance, but now he commands all people everywhere to repent. (Acts 17:30)

If my people, who are called by my name, will humble themselves and pray and seek my face and turn from their wicked ways, then will I hear from heaven and will forgive their sin and will heal their land. (2 Chr. 7:14)

Let the wicked forsake his way and the evil man his thoughts. Let him turn to the LORD, and he will have mercy on him, and to our God, for he will freely pardon. (Isa. 55:7)

"But if a wicked man turns away from all the sins he has committed and keeps all my decrees and does what is just and right, he will surely live; he will not die. (Ezek. 18:21)

K. Jacob's Faith: A Worshipping Faith, 11:21	
1. A faith that believed God's promises & worshipped despite death	21 By faith Jacob, when he was dying, blessed each of Joseph's sons, and worshiped as he leaned on the top of his staff.

DIVISION IV

THE SUPREME AUTHOR OF FAITH: JESUS CHRIST, GOD'S SON, 10:19–11:40

K. Jacob's Faith: A Worshipping Faith, 11:21

(11:21) **Introduction:** Jacob never saw the promised land given to Israel. In fact, he saw the reverse. His family was forced to Egypt because of famine. Yet he continued to worship God, ever believing and passing on God's promise—even as he was dying.

1 (11:21) **Jacob—Faith:** Jacob's faith was a faith that believed God's promises and worshipped despite death. The story in the Old Testament is as follows:

Some time later Joseph was told, "Your father is ill." So he took his two sons Manasseh and Ephraim along with him. When Jacob was told, "Your son Joseph has come to you," Israel rallied his strength and sat up on the bed. Jacob said to Joseph, "God Almighty appeared to me at Luz in the land of Canaan, and there he blessed me and said to me, 'I am going to make you fruitful and will increase your numbers. I will make you a community of peoples, and I will give this land as an everlasting possession to your descendants after you.' "Now then, your two sons born to you in Egypt before I came to you here will be reckoned as mine; Ephraim and Manasseh will be mine, just as Reuben and Simeon are mine. Any children born to you after them will be yours; in the territory they inherit they will be reckoned under the names of their brothers. And Joseph took both of them, Ephraim on his right toward Israel's left hand and Manasseh on his left toward Israel's right hand, and brought them close to him. But Israel reached out his right hand and put it on Ephraim's head, though he was the younger, and crossing his arms, he put his left hand on Manasseh's head, even though Manasseh was the firstborn. Then he blessed Joseph and said, "May the God before whom my fathers Abraham and Isaac walked, the God who has been my shepherd all my life to this day, the Angel who has delivered me from all harm—may he bless these boys. May they be called by my name and the names of my fathers Abraham and Isaac, and may they increase greatly upon the earth." (Gen. 48: 1–6, 13–16)

Note three significant facts.

1. Jacob was dying when this event took place. He had lived a long life upon earth.

2. Jacob blessed both of the sons of Joseph; that is, he passed on the promises of God to them. He gave them an inheritance in the *land of promise* and in the *promised seed*. They had been born in Egypt; nevertheless, he passed the blessing of the promise down through them.

3. Jacob worshipped while he was dying, worshipped leaning upon his staff. The idea is that he was weak and frail, almost bedridden, finding it difficult to walk and move about. But he continued to arise and worship God, believing in the *promised land* and *promised seed* up until the very end.

The point is striking. Here was a man who never saw the promised land given to him. In fact, he saw the reverse. He and his family were forced out of Canaan (Palestine) and into Egypt because of famine. Yet, he continued to worship God, ever believing and passing on God's promises—even up to the very end, the end of death itself.

So keep up your courage, men, for I have faith in God that it will happen just as he told me. (Acts 27:25)

And without faith it is impossible to please God, because anyone who comes to him must believe that he exists and that he rewards those who earnestly seek him. (Heb. 11:6)

In the same way, faith by itself, if it is not accompanied by action, is dead. (James 2:17)

The LORD redeems his servants; no one will be condemned who takes refuge in him. (Psa. 34:22)

Trust in the LORD and do good; dwell in the land and enjoy safe pasture. (Psa. 37:3)

Commit your way to the LORD; trust in him and he will do this: (Psa. 37:5)

Trust in the LORD with all your heart and lean not on your own understanding; (Prov. 3:5)

You will keep in perfect peace him whose mind is steadfast, because he trusts in you. Trust in the LORD forever, for the LORD, the LORD, is the Rock eternal. (Isa. 26:3–4)

	L. Joseph's Faith: An Undying Faith, 11:22
1 A faith that believed despite circumstances 2 A faith that acted despite the impossible	22 By faith Joseph, when his end was near, spoke about the exodus of the Israelites from Egypt and gave instructions about his bones.

DIVISION IV

THE SUPREME AUTHOR OF FAITH: JESUS CHRIST, GOD'S SON, 10:19–11:40

L. Joseph's Faith: An Undying Faith, 11:22

(11:22) Introduction: Joseph was a prince among a world of men. His life of faith is a life that should be studied and followed by all. The faith of Joseph was an undying faith.

1. A faith that believed despite circumstances (v. 22).
2. A faith that acted despite the impossible (v. 22).

1 (11:22) **Joseph—Faith:** Joseph's faith was faith that believed despite adverse circumstances. If ever a person should have lost faith, it was Joseph.

- ☞ As a young man, he had been sold as a slave into Egypt, and note: it was his own brothers who had sold him (Gen. 37:23f).
- ☞ While a slave, he was falsely accused by his master's wife of trying to seduce her. He had rejected her advances, choosing to follow God in living righteously rather than to enjoy the fruits of sin for a season (Gen. 39:7).
- ☞ He suffered imprisonment because the wife falsely charged him with assault. He suffered a long imprisonment for living righteously (Gen. 39:14f).
- ☞ He lived righteously and ministered to people in prison even when they ignored, neglected, and forgot him (Gen. 40:14f).

The point to note is this: Joseph never lost his faith in the promises of God. He believed and followed God no matter the circumstances and no matter what it cost him. He was a man of God in a foreign land, a man who demonstrated an undying faith.

2 (11:22) **Joseph—Faith:** Joseph had a faith that acted despite the impossible. This was Joseph's great act of faith. After so many years in a foreign land, he still proclaimed the great promise of God: he believed beyond question that God was going to fulfill His promises:

- ☞ He believed that God had chosen his family to be the *promised seed*.
- ☞ He believed that God was going to give the *promised land* to his family.

Joseph was dying in a foreign land with his family finally settled and rooted in the land of Goshen, Egypt. Yet he believed the impossible: that God would be moving his family back to Palestine and eventually give them the promised land. Therefore, he commanded that his bones be taken back when the nation of his family returned to the land.

Joseph's faith was an undying faith. His body was dying, but not his faith in God and in God's promises. He knew that he would rest in the promised land of God.

> **All men will hate you because of me, but he who stands firm to the end will be saved. (Matt. 10:22)**
>
> **If we live, we live to the Lord; and if we die, we die to the Lord. So, whether we live or die, we belong to the Lord. (Rom. 14:8)**
>
> **The one who sows to please his sinful nature, from that nature will reap destruction; the one who sows to please the Spirit, from the Spirit will reap eternal life. (Gal. 6:8)**
>
> **All these people were still living by faith when they died. They did not receive the things promised; they only saw them and welcomed them from a distance. And they admitted that they were aliens and strangers on earth. (Heb. 11:13)**
>
> **Therefore, get rid of all moral filth and the evil that is so prevalent and humbly accept the word planted in you, which can save you. (James 1:21)**
>
> **The Lord is not slow in keeping his promise, as some understand slowness. He is patient with you, not wanting anyone to perish, but everyone to come to repentance. (2 Pet. 3:9)**
>
> **Then I heard a voice from heaven say, "Write: Blessed are the dead who die in the Lord from now on." "Yes," says the Spirit, "they will rest from their labor, for their deeds will follow them." (Rev. 14:13)**
>
> **Even though I walk through the valley of the shadow of death, I will fear no evil, for you are with me; your rod and your staff, they comfort me. (Psa. 23:4)**
>
> **Precious in the sight of the LORD is the death of his saints. (Psa. 116:15)**
>
> **When calamity comes, the wicked are brought down, but even in death the righteous have a refuge. (Prov. 14:32)**

	M. Moses' Parent's Faith: A Loving, Fearless Faith, 11:23
1 A faith that obeyed their hearts	23 By faith Moses' parents hid him for three months after he was born, because they saw he was no ordinary child, and they were not afraid of the king's edict.
2 A faith that was fearless despite opposition	

DIVISION IV

THE SUPREME AUTHOR OF FAITH: JESUS CHRIST, GOD'S SON, 10:19–11:40

M. Moses' Parent's Faith: A Loving, Fearless Faith, 11:23

(11:23) Introduction: the parents of Moses are an excellent example of an unknown married couple who had great faith in God. They were just common, ordinary folk within their community, yet they believed God and had a strong faith in Him. Their faith stands as a dynamic example of a loving, fearless faith.

1. A faith that obeyed their hearts (v. 23).
2. A faith that was fearless despite opposition (v. 23).

1 (11:23) **Faith—Moses, Parents of:** the parents of Moses had a faith that obeyed their hearts. What happened was this. Generation after generation had passed since Joseph, Jacob, and his sons had gone down to Egypt and settled in the land of Goshen, Egypt. The people, the Israelites, had reproduced so much that they had become a large nation of people, so large that the new king of Egypt felt threatened by them. This was when Israel became slaves to the Egyptians. The king, who did not know Joseph, took the initial step of enslaving them, thinking that he could slow down their reproduction through slavery (Ex. 1:8). However, the children of Israel continued to multiply rather rapidly, and the king felt more and more threatened. Finally he decided to wipe them out by having all newborn sons killed at birth. This cruel plot was made the law of the land (cp. Ex. 1:21–22).

This is the background of what led Moses' parents to do what they did. Unquestionably, they loved God and loved their newborn child whom they named Moses. Their action shows this.

Kenneth Wuest points out that the words "no ordinary" (asteion) mean "comely to God." Wuest says, "he was comely with respect to God" (*Hebrews*, Vol. 2, p. 205). That is, God had His hand upon Moses, and apparently his parents realized it.

One thing is sure: the parents knew that if all the male children were killed, then the *promised seed* and *promised land* of God could never be fulfilled. It is this that lies behind their saving Moses. They loved their child, yes, but they also loved God. It was their love for both their son and God that made them do what they did. Their love stirred them to believe that God would preserve their son and use him to fulfill God's promise of an eternal seed and eternal land for His people.

Jesus replied: "'Love the Lord your God with all your heart and with all your soul and with all your mind.' (Matt. 22:37)

And so we know and rely on the love God has for us. God is love. Whoever lives in love lives in God, and God in him. (1 John 4:16)

Keep yourselves in God's love as you wait for the mercy of our Lord Jesus Christ to bring you to eternal life. (Jude 1:21)

Love the LORD your God with all your heart and with all your soul and with all your strength. (Deut. 6:5)

And now, O Israel, what does the LORD your God ask of you but to fear the LORD your God, to walk in all his ways, to love him, to serve the LORD your God with all your heart and with all your soul, (Deut. 10:12)

2 (11:23) **Faith—Moses, Parents of:** the parents of Moses had a faith that was fearless despite opposition. As stated above, it was the law of the land that all newborn male children were to be killed at birth. Failure to obey the law most likely meant death to the law-breaker. The parents risked their lives in disobeying the law. But note what this verse says: "they were not afraid of the king's edict." They trusted God to preserve the child, and they cast their own lives upon God's care. They knew they had to risk their lives in order to save their son and the promised seed and land of God.

The point is this: the parents of Moses never received the promised land of God and they never saw the promised seed inherit the land. But they believed and trusted God, even in the face of a king's attempt to stamp out God's people and promise. They loved God and His promises and they believed God and His promises; therefore, they were willing to stake their lives upon Him and *the promised seed and land.*

And without faith it is impossible to please God, because anyone who comes to him must believe that he exists and that he rewards those who earnestly seek him. (Heb. 11:6)

If any of you lacks wisdom, he should ask God, who gives generously to all without finding fault, and it will be given to him. But when he asks, he must believe and not doubt, because he who doubts is like a wave of the sea, blown and tossed by the wind. (James 1:5–6)

In the same way, faith by itself, if it is not accompanied by action, is dead. (James 2:17)

For everyone born of God overcomes the world. This is the victory that has overcome the world, even our faith. Who is it that overcomes the world? Only he who believes that Jesus is the Son of God. (1 John 5:4–5)

The LORD redeems his servants; no one will be condemned who takes refuge in him. (Psa. 34:22)

Commit your way to the LORD; trust in him and he will do this: (Psa. 37:5)

It is better to take refuge in the LORD than to trust in man. (Psa. 118:8)

Trust in the LORD with all your heart and lean not on your own understanding; (Prov. 3:5)

The rod of correction imparts wisdom, but a child left to himself disgraces his mother. (Prov. 29:15)

Trust in the LORD forever, for the LORD, the LORD, is the Rock eternal. (Isa. 26:4)

| 1 A sacrificial faith: He chose God & God's people rather than this world & its pleasures

2 An expectant faith: He | N. Moses' Faith: A Self-Denying Faith, 11:24-28

24 By faith Moses, when he had grown up, refused to be known as the son of Pharaoh's daughter.
25 He chose to be mistreated along with the people of God rather than to enjoy the pleasures of sin for a short time.
26 He regarded disgrace for the sake of Christ as of | greater value than the treasures of Egypt, because he was looking ahead to his reward.
27 By faith he left Egypt, not fearing the king's anger; he persevered because he saw him who is invisible.
28 By faith he kept the Passover and the sprinkling of blood, so that the destroyer of the firstborn would not touch the firstborn of Israel. | looked to the reward (v. 26, 27, 28)

3 An enduring faith: He courageously looked to God instead of looking to men
4 A saving faith: He believed God's message of salvation |

DIVISION IV

THE SUPREME AUTHOR OF FAITH: JESUS CHRIST, GOD'S SON, 10:19–11:40

N. Moses Faith: A Self-Denying Faith, 11:24–28

(11:24–28) **Introduction:** following Christ is not easy, not if a person is going to truly follow Him. Why? Because His call is contrary to what most people think. His call is a call to love, joy, and peace, yes; but it is not a call to a life of ease, comfort, and plenty. The call of Christ is not to physical and material health and wealth. Contrariwise, the call of Christ is to a life of self-denial and sacrifice. If a person is going to follow Christ, it costs him everything he is and has. And Christ makes no exceptions (see outline and notes—Mt. 19:16–22; 19:23–26; 19:27–30). Moses is a prime example of a man who gave up all that the world had to offer in order to follow God and His promises. His faith was a self-denying faith.

1. A sacrificial faith: he chose God and God's people rather than this world and its pleasures (v. 24–25).
2. An expectant faith: he looked to the reward (v. 26–28).
3. An enduring faith: he courageously looked to God instead of looking to man (v. 27).
4. A saving faith: he believed God's message of salvation (v. 28).

1 (11:24-25) **Moses—Faith:** first, the faith of Moses was a sacrificial faith, a faith that chose God and God's people rather than this world and its pleasures. Remember: when Moses was born, the king of Egypt had issued a law that all newborn male children of Israel were to be killed. He had done this because he feared Israel was growing so rapidly as a people that they were becoming a threat to the security of Egypt. The parents of Moses, acting in faith, had hid Moses down by the river in a small boat-like basket. Moses was only three months old. His parents knew that Pharaoh's daughter bathed there, and they sensed in hope that she would find the child, feel compassion, and keep and rear him. This she did. Moses was reared as a prince in Pharoah's court. Jewish tradition even says that his daughter was the only child Pharoah had and that she herself was childless. If this is accurate, it means that Moses was, as tradition says, the heir to the throne of Egypt (Thomas Hewitt. *The Epistle to the Hebrews.* "Tyndale New Testament Commentaries," p.180 and Matthew Henry. *Matthew Henry's Commentary*, Vol. 6, p. 947). In either case, Moses was a prince, the son of the daughter of Pharoah. He had everything that a person on earth could ever want:

⇨ education and knowledge
⇨ fame and wealth
⇨ possessions and estates
⇨ power and authority
⇨ position and duty
⇨ purpose and responsibility
⇨ a home and love (Pharoah's daughter must have loved Moses to stand against Egyptian law to save him as a child.)

But Moses gave it all up. He sacrificed everything for God and His promises, the *promised seed* and *promised land*. The day came when Moses had to make the most critical decision of his life. He faced as large a crisis as any man could face. Was he going to be identified as an Egyptian all the days of his life or was he going to become identified with the people of God? Was he going to pursue the pleasures of Egypt and this world or pursue God and His promises? When Moses was forty years old, he faced the crisis and made the decision (Acts 7:23). In the words of Scripture:

> **One day, after Moses had grown up, he went out to where his own people were and watched them at their hard labor. He saw an Egyptian beating a Hebrew, one of his own people. Glancing this way and that and seeing no one, he killed the Egyptian and hid him in the sand. (Exo. 2:11–12)**

This was a scene that Moses had often seen during his forty years as an Egyptian prince. But apparently this was the final straw; he had seen enough of the mistreatment of his people. He made the decision that launched a number of decisions—decisions that were to show that he was rejecting Egypt and the world and identifying himself with God's people.

The point is this: Moses gave up all the pleasures and enjoyment of Egypt and the world—gave it all up. He sacrificed everything for God and His people, the very people who had been given the hope for *the promised seed and the promised land.*

As these two verses of Hebrews say:

> **"[Aroused] by faith Moses, when he had grown to maturity and become great, refused**

to be called the son of Pharoah's daughter, because he preferred rather to share the oppression (suffer the hardships) and bear the shame of the people of God than to have the fleeting enjoyment of a sinful life" (v. 24-25, Amplified New Testament).

Thought 1. Moses knew what he was doing. The decision to do what he could to stop the abuse of God's people was not the rash decision of youth. Moses was forty years old, engaged in the midst of the daily duties and power of ruling. He made his decision and acted, but as the next verse shows, only after much thought.

Thought 2. The Expositor's Greek Testament has an excellent statement on this point: "the significance and source of this refusal lay in his preferring to suffer ill-usage with God's people rather than to have a short-lived enjoyment of sin. ... it was because they were God's people, not solely because they were of his blood, that Moses threw in his lot with them. It was this that illustrated his faith. He believed that God would fulfill His promise to His people, little likelihood as at present there seemed to be of any great future for his race. On the other hand there was...the enjoyment which was within his reach if only he committed the sin of denying his people and renouncing their future as promised by God" (Marcus Dods. *The Epistle to the Hebrews.* "The Expositor's Greek Testament," Vol. 14, ed. by W. Robertson Nicoll. Grand Rapids, MI: Eerdmans, 1970, p. 360).

> Then Jesus said to his disciples, "If anyone would come after me, he must deny himself and take up his cross and follow me. For whoever wants to save his life will lose it, but whoever loses his life for me will find it. (Matt. 16:24-25)
>
> Jesus answered, "If you want to be perfect, go, sell your possessions and give to the poor, and you will have treasure in heaven. Then come, follow me." (Matt. 19:21)
>
> In the same way, any of you who does not give up everything he has cannot be my disciple. (Luke 14:33)
>
> Nobody should seek his own good, but the good of others. (1 Cor. 10:24)
>
> For if you live according to the sinful nature, you will die; but if by the Spirit you put to death the misdeeds of the body, you will live, (Rom. 8:13)
>
> We who are strong ought to bear with the failings of the weak and not to please ourselves. (Rom. 15:1)

2 (11:26) **Moses—Faith:** second, the faith of Moses was an expectant faith, a faith that looked to the reward. Moses believed in the promises which God had given to Abraham and his people, the promised seed and the promised land. (See notes—Heb. 11:8-10; 11:13-16 for more discussion.) The word "regarded" means that he considered and thought about the matter; he made a deliberate decision to suffer with his people and to inherit the promises God had made to them rather than to enjoy the riches of Egypt. This means ...

- that he chose the sufferings of Christ, the promised seed of the Savior, over the riches of Egypt.
- that he considered the reward of God's promise to Israel greater than the reward of earthly riches.

William Barclay explains what Moses did in practical terms:

> "Moses was the man who gave up all earthly glory for the sake of the people of God. Christ gave up His glory for men. He became despised and rejected; He abandoned the glory of heaven for the buffets and the scourging and the shame inflicted by men. Moses in his day and generation shared in the sufferings of Christ. Moses was the man who chose the loyalty that led to suffering rather than the ease which led to earthly glory. He would rather suffer for the right than enjoy luxury with the wrong. He knew that the prizes of earth were contemptible compared with the ultimate reward of God" (The Letter to the Hebrews, p. 178)

Without question, Moses believed in the promises of God to Israel:

- that Israel was the promised seed, the very people through whom God would send the Messiah, the Savior of the world.
- that Israel would inherit the promised land of eternal rest with God. Moses turned away from the riches of the world for the rewards of God's promises.

> **"He considered the contempt and abuse and shame [borne for] the Christ, the Messiah [Who was to come], to be greater wealth than all the treasures of Egypt, for he looked forward and away to the reward (recompense)"** (v. 26, Amplified New Testament).
>
> **"Blessed are you when people insult you, persecute you and falsely say all kinds of evil against you because of me. (Matt. 5:11)**
>
> **And if anyone gives even a cup of cold water to one of these little ones because he is my disciple, I tell you the truth, he will certainly not lose his reward." (Matt. 10:42)**
>
> **If we endure, we will also reign with him. If we disown him, he will also disown us; (2 Tim. 2:12)**
>
> **You sympathized with those in prison and joyfully accepted the confiscation of your property, because you knew that you yourselves had better and lasting possessions. (Heb. 10:34)**
>
> **Some faced jeers and flogging, while still others were chained and put in prison. (Heb 11:36)**

3 (11:27) **Moses—Faith:** third, the faith of Moses was an enduring faith, a faith that courageously looked to God rather than to men. This event is recorded in Exodus.

> **The next day he went out and saw two Hebrews fighting. He asked the one in the wrong, "Why are you hitting your fellow Hebrew?" The man said, "Who made you ruler and judge over us? Are you thinking of killing me as you killed the Egyptian?" Then Moses**

was afraid and thought, "What I did must have become known." When Pharaoh heard of this, he tried to kill Moses, but Moses fled from Pharaoh and went to live in Midian, where he sat down by a well. (Exo. 2:13–15)

Note: it seems that Moses fled because he feared Pharoah; however, Hebrews says that he "left Egypt, not fearing the kings' anger." Is this a contradiction? No, the answer is given in Acts:

"When Moses was forty years old, he decided to visit his fellow Israelites. He saw one of them being mistreated by an Egyptian, so he went to his defense and avenged him by killing the Egyptian. Moses thought that his own people would realize that God was using him to rescue them, but they did not. (Acts 7:23–25)

This shows that Moses had apparently thought and known for years that he was to be the deliverer of Israel. It is highly probable that his own mother had taught him this when Pharoah's daughter unknowingly made her the nurse to Moses (Ex. 2:6–8). She certainly taught him the great promises of God to Abraham and Israel. Whatever the source, God's Spirit apparently moved upon Moses at an early age and stirred the sense and thoughts that he was to be the deliverer of his people; he was to lead them back to Israel. However, Moses went about it the wrong way. Nevertheless, he knew that God's will and purpose was for him to deliver his people. Note: Acts 7:25 says that Moses was planning to lead Israel in a rebellion against Egypt to free God's people. He did not fear Pharoah; Moses was loaded with courage. However, when the people refused to follow him, he was left alone. He had to fear—fear in the sense of wisdom and discretion, not despondency and hopelessness. He had to fear in order to save his life.

The point is this: Moses sensed and knew his mission upon earth—that he was to free Israel in God's time. The people would not follow him then, but he believed that God would arouse the people to follow him in due time. As we find out, he kept on believing and endured in his belief for another forty years (Acts 7:30).

Thought 1. Imagine the terrible disappointment Moses must have felt. His people were suffering as slave-laborers under Egyptian bondage, and he had stepped forward to lead them in a rebellion for freedom. But they had rejected his leadership, and he had been forced to flee for his life. The disappointment must have been very heavy. But imagine this: Moses sensed and knew that God had called him to deliver His people Israel. He knew his calling. But there he was sitting in Midian, and he had sat there for forty years and God had not called him to go forth. How easily Moses could have lost faith in God. How easily he could have lost his sense of call. But he did not: he continued to believe in God and His promises. Moses endured in faith despite all the circumstances. What a dynamic example!

Therefore, my dear brothers, stand firm. Let nothing move you. Always give yourselves fully to the work of the Lord, because you know that your labor in the Lord is not in vain. (1 Cor. 15:58)

Let us not become weary in doing good, for at the proper time we will reap a harvest if we do not give up. (Gal. 6:9)

Therefore, since we have a great high priest who has gone through the heavens, Jesus the Son of God, let us hold firmly to the faith we profess. For we do not have a high priest who is unable to sympathize with our weaknesses, but we have one who has been tempted in every way, just as we are—yet was without sin. Let us then pproach the throne of grace with confidence, so that we may receive mercy and find grace to help us in our time of need. (Heb. 4:14–16)

Let us hold unswervingly to the hope we profess, for he who promised is faithful. (Heb. 10:23)

Therefore, prepare your minds for action; be self-controlled; set your hope fully on the grace to be given you when Jesus Christ is revealed. (1 Pet. 1:13)

I am coming soon. Hold on to what you have, so that no one will take your crown. (Rev. 3:11)

4 (11:28) **Moses—Faith:** fourth, the faith of Moses was a saving faith, a faith that believed God's message of salvation. This verse refers to the great day of deliverance and salvation for Israel. God had led Moses to prepare Israel and Egypt for the deliverance of His people. God was now ready to save His people from the bondage of Egypt (a symbol of the world). God had pronounced judgment (the taking of the firstborn) upon the people of Egypt for their injustices. As He prepared to execute the final judgment, those who believed God were instructed to slay a pure lamb and sprinkle its blood over the door posts of their homes. The blood of the innocent lamb would then serve as a sign that the coming judgment had already been carried out. When seeing the blood, God would *pass over* that house.

Symbolically, the Passover pictured the coming of Jesus Christ as the Savior. The lamb without blemish pictured His sinless life, and the blood sprinkled on the door posts pictured His blood shed for the believer (Ex. 12:5; cp. Jn. 1:29).

Note that God's method of salvation was the blood of the lamb spread over the door posts (cp. Gen. 12:12–48. See DEEPER STUDY # 1—Lk. 22:7.) Moses' great faith is clearly seen. He not only made the proper arrangements for escaping God's judgment on that dreadful night, but he spelled out that the Passover was to be observed each year thereafter. He never doubted God's planned salvation for His people. He never doubted that God would fulfill His promises, that He would give to Israel the *promised seed* and the *promised land*.

Since we have now been justified by his blood, how much more shall we be saved from God's wrath through him! (Rom. 5:9)

For, "Everyone who calls on the name of the Lord will be saved." (Rom. 5:9)

For it is by grace you have been saved, through faith—and this not from yourselves, it is the gift of God—(Eph. 2:8)

In fact, the law requires that nearly everything be cleansed with blood, and without the shedding of blood there is no forgiveness. (Heb. 9:22)

For you know that it was not with perishable things such as silver or gold that you were redeemed from the empty way of life handed down to you from your forefathers, but with the precious blood of Christ, a lamb without blemish or defect. (1 Pet. 1:18–19)

	O. Israel's Faith (Part I): A Delivering Faith, 11:29
1 A faith that obeyed God against insurmountable forces 2 A faith that delivered & brought protection	29 By faith the people passed through the Red Sea as on dry land; but when the Egyptians tried to do so, they were drowned.

DIVISION IV

THE SUPREME AUTHOR OF FAITH: JESUS CHRIST, GOD'S SON, 10:19–11:40

O. Israel's Faith (Part I): A Delivering Faith, 11:29

(11:29) **Introduction:** this verse deals with Israel crossing the Red Sea, a phenomenal miracle controlled entirely by God. But it took great faith for Israel to cross the Sea with two towering walls of water on both sides. This is a living example of strong faith in God, a delivering faith, the kind of faith that assures God's delivering power acting in our behalf.

    1. A faith that obeyed God against insurmountable forces (v. 29).
    2. A faith that delivered and brought protection (v. 29).

1 (11:29) **Israel—Faith:** Israel's faith was a faith that obeyed God against insurmountable forces. The forces confronting Israel were threefold:

- the pursuing army of the Egyptians.
- the Red Sea in front and the mountain ranges on both sides.
- their own murmuring and unbelief.

The people were ever so frightened. They were hemmed in with no way to escape, and an enraged king and people were in hot pursuit. There was no chance that the Egyptian army would have taken any live prisoners because Egypt had lost all their firstborn sons to the death-angel. Israel was doomed and the people knew it. The odds were insurmountable unless God stepped in and delivered them.

Moses, God's leader, was aroused to believe God. He stepped forward and shouted to the people:

> **Moses answered the people, "Do not be afraid. Stand firm and you will see the deliverance the LORD will bring you today. The Egyptians you see today you will never see again. The LORD will fight for you; you need only to be still." (Exo. 14:13–14)**

The salvation of the Lord was being proclaimed, and that message stirred faith in the hearts of the people. In obedience to God's command, Moses lifted up his rod and moved it across the face of the waters. When he did, a strong east wind began to blow over the face of the water. It blew so forcefully that the waters divided. Imagine the scene: two towering walls of water with a stretch of dry land running down between them. But the people's salvation was on the other side. If they could reach there, they were safe. They had been grumbling, yes; but the message of God's servant, Moses, had stirred them to believe God. Now they were beholding the power of God to remove the insurmountable

odds. He had actually rolled the sea back and made a road of *dry land* for them to march across to safety. They believed God, and they began to march forth—marching in the faith of God who had promised that He would lead them to the promised land.

Thought 1. What a clear picture of salvation for people today! No matter the odds, God will overcome the odds and save us if we will only believe and begin to march forth following Christ, even as God commands.

> **Jesus replied, "I tell you the truth, if you have faith and do not doubt, not only can you do what was done to the fig tree, but also you can say to this mountain, 'Go, throw yourself into the sea,' and it will be done. (Matt. 21:21)**
>
> **No temptation has seized you except what is common to man. And God is faithful; he will not let you be tempted beyond what you can bear. But when you are tempted, he will also provide a way out so that you can stand up under it. (1 Cor. 10:13)**
>
> **He has delivered us from such a deadly peril, and he will deliver us. On him we have set our hope that he will continue to deliver us, (2 Cor. 1:10)**
>
> **The Lord will rescue me from every evil attack and will bring me safely to his heavenly kingdom. To him be glory for ever and ever. Amen. (2 Tim. 4:18)**
>
> **Since the children have flesh and blood, he too shared in their humanity so that by his death he might destroy him who holds the power of death—that is, the devil—and free those who all their lives were held in slavery by their fear of death. (Heb. 2:14–15)**
>
> **If this is so, then the Lord knows how to rescue godly men from trials and to hold the unrighteous for the day of judgment, while continuing their punishment. (2 Pet. 2:9)**
>
> **The LORD is my strength and my shield; my heart trusts in him, and I am helped. My heart leaps for joy and I will give thanks to him in song. (Psa. 28:7)**
>
> **Yet I am poor and needy; may the Lord think of me. You are my help and my deliverer; O my God, do not delay. (Psa. 40:17)**

2 (11:29) **Israel—Faith:** Israel's faith was a faith that delivered and brought protection. The people believed God; therefore, they were delivered despite the insurmountable odds against them. But not only this: they were protected through the whole experience. Their enemies pursued them. It was night when Israel crossed the sea and when the Egyptian army reached the shore (Ex. 14:21). The Egyptians were spiritually blind to God's working and were hardened in their sin. After all, the children of Israel were not an army, but a defenseless body of people fleeing the might and power of the greatest army in the world. The Egyptians saw no reason to rush behind the people of Israel and slaughter them. Therefore, the army acted blindly, rashly, and unthoughtfully. They went right in after Israel. But God protected those who believed and trusted Him. The east wind died down and the two walls of water closed in and covered the pursuing enemy, drowning every one of them. God's people were protected—completely protected by the hand of God.

> **Thought 1.** God performed the miracle of salvation and deliverance for the people, but it was because of their faith. God's messenger proclaimed the salvation of God and the people believed and God worked in their behalf. He saved and protected them from their enemy—an enemy that had appeared insurmountable. God always provides a way of deliverance for those who believe.
>
> **Jesus replied, "I tell you the truth, if you have faith and do not doubt, not only can you do what was done to the fig tree, but also you can say to this mountain, 'Go, throw yourself into the sea,' and it will be done. (Matt. 21:21)**
>
> **"For God so loved the world that he gave his one and only Son, that whoever believes in him shall not perish but have eternal life. (John 3:16)**
>
> **And everyone who calls on the name of the Lord will be saved.' (Acts 2:21)**
>
> **For, "Everyone who calls on the name of the Lord will be saved." (Rom. 10:13)**
>
> **For it is by grace you have been saved, through faith—and this not from yourselves, it is the gift of God—not by works, so that no one can boast. (Eph. 2:8–9)**
>
> **The salvation of the righteous comes from the LORD; he is their stronghold in time of trouble. (Psa. 37:39)**
>
> **Surely God is my salvation; I will trust and not be afraid. The LORD, the LORD, is my strength and my song; he has become my salvation." (Isa. 12:2)**
>
> **In that day they will say, "Surely this is our God; we trusted in him, and he saved us. This is the LORD, we trusted in him; let us rejoice and be glad in his salvation." (Isa. 25:9)**
>
> **The LORD your God is with you, he is mighty to save. He will take great delight in you, he will quiet you with his love, he will rejoice over you with singing." (Zeph. 3:17)**

	P. Israel's Faith (Part II): A Conquering Faith, 11:30
1. A faith that believed the unusual: At Jericho	30 By faith the walls of Jericho fell, after the people had marched around them for seven days.

DIVISION IV

THE SUPREME AUTHOR OF FAITH: JESUS CHRIST, GOD'S SON, 10:19–11:40

P. Israel's Faith (Part II): A Conquering Faith, 11:30

(11:30) **Introduction:** the faith of Israel was a conquering faith. This was the kind of faith Israel needed in conquering Jericho—a faith that God could give victory over insurmountable forces (cp. Ex. 14:1f). This is also the kind of faith that any person needs—a conquering faith. We need a faith that God will give us victory over the insurmountable forces of life no matter what the forces are, even the force of death.

1 (11:30) **Israel—Faith:** Israel's faith was a conquering faith. This is the story of Joshua leading the people of Israel against Jericho (Josh. 6:1–20). The fall of the walls of Jericho is a well-known story. Jericho was a fortress, completely surrounded by a wall and apparently manned by a strong people. How was Israel to take the city? Humanly speaking, the task was utterly impossible. Their only hope was God, and God was willing to give them victory over their enemies. It was just a matter of whether or not they would believe and trust God for victory. God issued His command:

- ✏ The people were to march around the walls of Jericho once a day for six days.
- ✏ Seven priests were to lead the march with the ark of the covenant following and then the people following it.
- ✏ The march was to be in total silence for six days.
- ✏ On the seventh day, the people were to march around the city seven times. After the seventh march, the priests were to blow seven trumpets and the people were to shout as loud as they could.

God said that if the people did this—believed His instructions and His promise—the walls of Jericho would fall down. Of course most of the citizens of Jericho would be on top of the wall because of the change of events on the seventh day, expecting this to be the day that Israel was going to attack.

The point to see is the strong faith in God and in His instructions and promise. The people clearly trusted God to conquer their enemies for them. And He did. He conquered the enemies because the people believed His instructions and promise.

Thought 1. God will conquer the enemies of any person if the person will just believe the instructions and promise of God. The instruction may seem unreasonable and appear foolish to the world. What Israel did must have seemed very foolish to the citizens of Jericho. But if a person will go ahead and do what God says, God will conquer his enemies even as He did for Jericho.

What, then, shall we say in response to this? If God is for us, who can be against us? He who did not spare his own Son, but gave him up for us all—how will he not also, along with him, graciously give us all things? Who will bring any charge against those whom God has chosen? It is God who justifies. Who is he that condemns? Christ Jesus, who died—more than that, who was raised to life—is at the right hand of God and is also interceding for us. Who shall separate us from the love of Christ? Shall trouble or hardship or persecution or famine or nakedness or danger or sword? As it is written: "For your sake we face death all day long; we are considered as sheep to be slaughtered." No, in all these things we are more than conquerors through him who loved us. For I am convinced that neither death nor life, neither angels nor demons, neither the present nor the future, nor any powers, neither height nor depth, nor anything else in all creation, will be able to separate us from the love of God that is in Christ Jesus our Lord. (Rom. 8:31–39)

But thanks be to God, who always leads us in triumphal procession in Christ and through us spreads everywhere the fragrance of the knowledge of him. (2 Cor. 2:14)

Since the children have flesh and blood, he too shared in their humanity so that by his death he might destroy him who holds the power of death—that is, the devil—and free those who all their lives were held in slavery by their fear of death. (Heb. 2:14–15)

For everyone born of God overcomes the world. This is the victory that has overcome the world, even our faith. Who is it that overcomes the world? Only he who believes that Jesus is the Son of God. (1 John 5:4–5)

Through you we push back our enemies; through your name we trample our foes. (Psa. 44:5)

The God of peace will soon crush Satan under your feet. The grace of our Lord Jesus be with you. (Rom. 16:20)

No temptation has seized you except what is common to man. And God is faithful; he will not let you be tempted beyond what you can bear. But when you are tempted, he will also provide a way out so that you can stand up under it. (1 Cor. 10:13)

Submit yourselves, then, to God. Resist the devil, and he will flee from you. (James 4:7)

To him who overcomes, I will give the right to sit with me on my throne, just as I overcame and sat down with my Father on his throne. (Rev. 3:21)

	Q. Rahab's Faith: A Saving Faith, 11:31
1 A faith that believed in the God of Israel 2 A faith that saved	31 By faith the prostitute Rahab, because she welcomed the spies, was not killed with those who were disobedient.

DIVISION IV

THE SUPREME AUTHOR OF FAITH: JESUS CHRIST, GOD'S SON, 10:19–11:40

Q. Rahab's Faith: A Saving Faith, 11:31

(11:31) **Introduction:** this is a beautiful picture of saving faith. It is the picture of one of Christ's ancestors, the picture of a harlot who turned from her sin to live for God. And because she did, she was saved and became one of the great women of history in the eyes of God and believers everywhere.

1. A faith that believed in the God of Israel (v. 31).
2. A faith that saved (v. 31).

1 (11:31) **Rahab—Faith:** the faith of Rahab was a faith that believed in the God of Israel (cp. Josh. 2:1–21; 6:17, 22–23, 25; Mt. 1:5; Jas. 2:25). She was a harlot and a Canaanite, a woman who was the furthest thing from being a follower of God, but she experienced a phenomenal conversion and she became a strong believer. What happened was this.

Joshua sent two spies into Jericho to spy out the city. They were almost caught, but they found refuge in the house of a prostitute named Rahab. The armed soldiers had heard that the spies were hiding out in her house and they confronted her, but she hid and protected them. Why? Why would she lie to her people and protect the two Israelite strangers? Scripture says because she believed in the God of Israel. How could she have possibly believed in the God of Israel when she was not an Israelite and had never been taught about the God of Israel and His promises? Scripture tells us. In conversation with the two spies she said:

> And said to them, "I know that the LORD has given this land to you and that a great fear of you has fallen on us, so that all who live in this country are melting in fear because of you. We have heard how the LORD dried up the water of the Red Sea for you when you came out of Egypt, and what you did to Sihon and Og, the two kings of the Amorites east of the Jordan, whom you completely destroyed. When we heard of it, our hearts melted and everyone's courage failed because of you, for the LORD your God is God in heaven above and on the earth below. (Josh. 2:9–11)

Rahab believed what she had heard about the God of Israel—that He was the true and living God. When it was humanly impossible for Israel to conquer Jericho—when Israel had no modern weapons to make war—when there was not a chance in this world that Israel could be victorious—Rahab believed in the God of Israel and she acted upon that faith. She believed that the God of Israel would save His people and give them the promised land. Therefore, she saved the lives of the two Israelite spies.

> How great is your **goodness, which you have stored up for those who fear you, which you bestow in the sight of men on those who take refuge in you. (Psa. 31:19)**
> Many are the woes of the wicked, but the **Lord's unfailing love surrounds the man who trusts in him. (Psa. 32:10)**
> The LORD **redeems his servants; no one will be condemned who takes refuge in him. (Psa. 34:22)**
> Commit your way to the LORD; **trust in him and he will do this: (Psa. 37:5)**
> It is better to take refuge in the **LORD than to trust in man. (Psa. 118:8)**
> Trust in the LORD with all your **heart and lean not on your own understanding; (Prov. 3:5)**
> Fear of man will prove to be a snare, but **whoever trusts in the LORD is kept safe. (Prov. 29:25)**
> Who among you fears the LORD and obeys **the word of his servant? Let him who walks in the dark, who has no light, trust in the name of the LORD and rely on his God. (Isa. 50:10)**

2 (11:31) **Rahab—Faith:** the faith of Rahab was a faith that saved her and her family. Rahab asked the two men to save her and her family when they attacked the city.

> Now then, please swear to me by the LORD **that you will show kindness to my family, because I have shown kindness to you. Give me a sure sign that you will spare the lives of my father and mother, my brothers and sisters, and all who belong to them, and that you will save us from death." "Our lives for your lives!" the men assured her. "If you don't tell what we are doing, we will treat you kindly and faithfully when the LORD gives us the land." So she let them down by a rope through the window, for the house she lived in was part of the city wall. Now she had said to them, "Go to the hills so**

the pursuers will not find you. Hide yourselves there three days until they return, and then go on your way." The men said to her, "This oath you made us swear will not be binding on us unless, when we enter the land, you have tied this scarlet cord in the window through which you let us down, and unless you have brought your father and mother, your brothers and all your family into your house. If anyone goes outside your house into the street, his blood will be on his own head; we will not be responsible. As for anyone who is in the house with you, his blood will be o our head if a hand is laid on him. But if you tell what we are doing, we will be released from the oath you made us swear." "Agreed," she replied. "Let it be as you say." So she sent them away and they departed. And she tied the scarlet cord in the window. (Josh. 2:12–21)

Note: it was seeing the scarlet (red) thread that was to save Rahab. Also note that Rahab demanded that the men "swear to her by the Lord." She strongly believed that Israel would conquer Jericho despite the impossible odds against them. She believed in the God of Israel: that God was going to give Israel the promised land. And most important of all, she believed that her life and salvation rested with the Israelites, that is, with the God of Israel. She believed that the God of Israel could and would save her. Oliver Greene has an excellent picture on the scarlet thread and salvation:

"This presents a beautiful picture of salvation. Two spies made the promise, Rahab believed it; and even though a great host of Israelites were to move in upon the city, she believed that the scarlet thread was her assurance of protection. All the money in Jericho could not have purchased that scarlet thread, because it was Rahab's guarantee of preservation while others were destroyed through unbelief: 'And Joshua saved Rahab the harlot alive, and her father's household, and all that she had; and she dwelleth in Israel even unto this day; because she hid the messengers, which Joshua sent to spy out Jericho' (Josh. 6:25).

"This is most interesting. The Word of God does not name the Israelites who befriended this woman of Jericho, but some noble soul in the land of Israel took her in, loved her, and gave her a new home; and as she lived among the Israelites she grew in grace, in faith, and in strength.

"We can easily believe that Rahab was an attractive woman, one who had a winning personality and the ability to make friends easily; but now she had something more: she had the Lord God in her heart. She was a new creation, a completely new woman.

"A young man in Israel fell in love with her and married her. (I like to think that this young man was one of the spies, but that is just supposition on my part. The Bible does not tell us who he was.) The record does prove, however, that Rahab became the wife of an Israelite and God blessed them, gave them a son, and they called his name Boaz.

"We read of Boaz in Ruth 2:1 that he was a 'mighty man of wealth,' and Matthew 1:5 tells us, 'Salmon begat Booz (Boaz) of Rachab; and Booz begat Obed of Ruth; and Obed begat Jesse.' Jesse was the father of David, and it was through the lineage of David that the Saviour came!

"You see, when God saves a harlot, a murderer, a liar, a thief - or even a good moral person, that one becomes a new creation with a new heart and a new life. God saves - He does not repair: 'Therefore if any man be in Christ, he is a new creature: old things are passed away; behold, all things are become new' (II Cor. 5:17)" (The Epistle of Paul the Apostle to the Hebrews, p. 504f).

Thought 1. Just imagine! Rahab was one of the human ancestors of the Savior Himself, Christ Jesus our Lord. What a glorious picture of the saving grace of God. And His mercy and grace are eternal: they are able to save any of us today no matter how much of a harlot, derelict, thief, murderer, adulterer, liar, fame-seeker, drug addict, leader, boaster, socialite, or materialist we are. Whether we would be considered to be down and out or of the upper crust within society, God can save us. No matter what we are or what we have done, God can save us if we will only believe and trust in His Son, the Lord Jesus Christ.

That everyone who believes in him may have eternal life. "For God so loved the world that he gave his one and only Son, that whoever believes in him shall not perish but have eternal life. (John 3:15–16)

Whoever believes in the Son has eternal life, but whoever rejects the Son will not see life, for God's wrath remains on him." (John 3:36)

"I tell you the truth, whoever hears my word and believes him who sent me has eternal life and will not be condemned; he has crossed over from death to life. (John 5:24)

Jesus said to her, "I am the resurrection and the life. He who believes in me will live, even though he dies; (John 11:25)

I have come into the world as a light, so that no one who believes in me should stay in darkness. (John 12:46)

But these are written that you may believe that Jesus is the Christ, the Son of God, and that by believing you may have life in his name. (John 20:31)

That if you confess with your mouth, "Jesus is Lord," and believe in your heart that God raised him from the dead, you will be saved. For it is with your heart that you believe and are justified, and it is with your mouth that you confess and are saved. (Rom. 10:9–10)

And how from infancy you have known the holy Scriptures, which are able to make you wise for salvation through faith in Christ Jesus. (2 Tim. 3:15)

	R. The Great Believers' Faith (Part I): A Heroic Faith, 11:32-34
1 The heroic faith of out-standing leaders: A faith that accepted incredible responsibility & that called upon God for great courage 2 The reward of heroic faith a. Conversed kingdoms b. Ruled with justice c. Obtained promises d. Shut the mouth of lions, v. 33 e. Quenched fire f. Escaped the sword g. Grew powerful in battle h. Routed armies	32 And what more shall I say? I do not have time to tell about Gideon, Barak, Samson, Jephthah, David, Samuel and the prophets, 33 Who through faith conquered kingdoms, administered justice, and gained what was promised; who shut the mouths of lions, 34 Quenched the fury of the flames, and escaped the edge of the sword; whose weakness was turned to strength; and who became powerful in battle and routed foreign armies.

DIVISION IV

THE SUPREME AUTHOR OF FAITH: JESUS CHRIST, GOD'S SON, 10:19–11:40

R. The Great Believers' Faith (Part I): A Heroic Faith, 11:32–34

(11:32–34) **Introduction:** heroic faith—this is a powerful picture of just what heroic faith is. It is a panoramic scene that glances back over the history of Israel highlighting the lives of some great men of faith—men who dared to believe God against unbelievable odds. And in every case their faith triumphed and won the victory.

1. The heroic faith of outstanding leaders: a faith that accepted incredible responsibility and that called upon God for great courage (v. 32).
2. The reward of heroic faith (v. 33–34).

1 (11:32) **Faith—Hall of Fame:** the heroic faith of out-standing leaders. Note that these three verses discuss the faith of some outstanding leaders. The faith of believers in general is discussed in the next few verses (v.35-40). These particular leaders were true heroes of the faith. They had a faith …

* that led them to feel undeserving and that demon strated humility.
* that accepted incredible responsibility.
* that showed undying courage.
* that trusted and depended entirely upon God.
* that conquered against all odds—unbelievable odds.

1. There was the faith of Gideon (Judg. 6:11f). Gideon was already a grown man when God called him (Judg. 8:20), and he had apparently gained a reputation as a soldier by fighting against the terrorists acts of the Medianites (Judg. 6:12). The terrorists' attacks against Israel had gotten so fierce and fre-quent that the people had to be on constant guard. They even had to work inside protective walls in order to get their work

done (Judg. 6:11). Note these facts:

* The angel of the Lord called Gideon to take the lead and to save Israel.
* Gideon felt unqualified. He was gripped with a sense of humility and unworthiness. However, God gave Gideon assurance after assurance.
* Gideon finally believed God and God gave Gideon the Spirit of the Lord.
* Gideon tested God's call and promise by putting out the well known test of the fleece (Judg. 6:36–40). God again assured Gideon that he was His chosen vessel to save Israel.
* Gideon believed God, and with three hundred hand-picked men he defied incredible odds and routed and defeated the Medianite army (Judg. 7:1f).

The point is this: Gideon was an outstanding leader because of his great faith. Even before he launched the great campaign against the Medianites, he cried out to his three hundred hand-picked men: "Get up! The Lord has given the Midianite camp into your hands" (Judg. 7:15).

2. There was the heroic faith of Barak (Judg. 4–5). When the call of God came to Barak to save Israel, the Canaanites had been attacking and oppressing Israel for twenty years. The com-mander-in-chief of the Canaanite army was Sisero. Note these facts:

* The call of God to Barak came through the prophetess Deborah.
* Barak was already a soldier, but he hesitated, feeling incapable. He insisted that the prophetess of God go to battle by his side. When she agreed, he surrendered to God's call.

- Barak faced incredible odds. Sisero, the commander-in-chief of the Canaanites, had over 900 chariots of iron and a massive army.
- Barak believed God. He attacked with only 10,000 men and won an incredible victory.

How did Barak do it? By faith. He had a heroic faith in God. He did not act without God. He believed God, and because he believed, God gave him the victory.

3. There was the heroic faith of Samson (Judg. 13–16). The angel of the Lord appeared to the mother of Samson and told her that she was to bear a son who was to save Israel from the Philistines. Samson was to be reared under the Nazarite vows of extreme discipline, self-denial, and control of the sinful nature. The purpose of the Nazarite vows was symbolic, to teach the people that they were to live lives of self-denial and dedication before God. Note these facts about Samson.

- Samson was appointed by God and he was a devout servant of God: "the Spirit of the Lord began to stir him" (Judg.13:25; cp. Judg.14:19).
- Samson was a man who had a serious flaw and weakness throughout all of his life, a weakness of fleshly passion. He never repented of his fleshly passion nor did he live by his Nazarite vows, not consistently.
- Samson was a man of unusual faith and courage. He single-handedly fought the Philistines with unbelievable exploits of strength time and again. And he always won the victory.

The point to note about Samson's life is this: despite Samson's life-long weakness of passion, when the time came, he alone believed God; he alone was available for God to use. Samson was sometimes weak and passionate, but all others were even weaker and had less if any faith. Samson alone was available to believe and trust God. He was a man of heroic faith.

Thought 1. Matthew Henry makes a statement that we must always realize: "True faith is acknowledged and accepted, even when mingled with many failings" (*Matthew Henry's Commentary*, Vol. 6, p. 951).

4. There was the heroic faith of Jephthah (Judg. 11:1–12:7). Jephthah was called by God to save Israel from the Ammonites. Note these significant facts.

- Jephthah was a man who had known rejection all of his life. He was the son of a harlot, but he was taken and reared by his father. However, he was apparently rejected, taunted, and abused by his family and neighbors all during his childhood. He was finally driven away from his home into the desert in exile (Judg. 11:1–3). There in the desert he became the leader of a group of fighting adventurers who protected surrounding villages from Ammonite terrorists.
- Jephthah believed and accepted the call to fight and save Israel when it came (Judg. 11:4-11). He made a covenant with the elders of his people "before the Lord" (Judg. 11:11).
- Jephthah sought God's presence and strength for victory by making a vow to God (Josh. 11:30–31).

- Jephthah did what God wanted him to do and saved Israel (Josh. 11:33).
- Jephthah kept his vow to God and had his daughter live as a virgin and dedicate her life to serve God.

The point to see is that Jephthah was a man of unusual faith and trust in God despite being rejected by his family and townsfolk. He was also a man of great humility who humbled himself to help save and rule the people in their great crisis. Jephthah was a man of heroic faith.

5. There was the heroic faith of David (1 Sam. 16:1f). As the writer to Hebrews says, "I do not have time to tell ... about David" (v. 32). David was unquestionably one of the greatest men of heroic faith who has ever lived. Note these facts:

- David was chosen to be the King of Israel by God Himself when he was only a young shepherd boy (1 Sam. 16:1f).

From that day on the Spirit of the Lord came upon David in power. (1 Sam. 16:13)

- David was *a boy of heroic faith*. He believed God in facing impossible situations. For example, a lion and a bear attacked his sheep and a giant of a man named Goliath led the Philistine army against Israel, but God honored the young boy's faith and gave David the victory in both situations.
- David was *a young man of heroic faith*. He was feared and hated by Saul the King because he had been appointed to be the future king of Israel while only a young boy. Saul pursued David for years trying to kill him. David proved to be a young man of extraordinary trust in God as he lived in the wilderness and faced trial after trial and enemy after enemy.
- David was *a man of heroic faith* in defeating enemy after enemy. He stretched the borders of Israel out farther than anyone else had ever done and brought Israel to the height of its glory as a nation.
- David ruled Israel for forty years and proved *faithful throughout his whole life* with exception of the one or two year lapse with Bathsheba (2 Sam. 11:1f).

The whole life of David is a challenging example of heroic faith to believers of every generation. Just think of the Psalms, how meaningful they are to us all. David wrote approximately 73 of the Psalms. He was also one of the ancestors of Christ (Mt. 1:1).

6. There was the heroic faith of Samuel (1–2 Samuel). Samuel was both a judge and prophet of Israel. God called Samuel when he was only a young child, and Samuel followed the Lord all through his life. During his lifetime he was the lone figure of great faith among a people who rebelled against God and refused to follow Him in righteousness and holiness. He was a man of heroic faith in the midst of a faithless and unbelieving generation.

7. There was the heroic faith of the prophets. They were all men who sensed their unworthiness before God but who answered God's call. They faced every imaginable trial that can be thrown against a man by a wicked and sinful people. But despite all, they stood for righteousness and proclaimed the message of God, a message of hope for those who would repent

and a message of judgment for those who continued to live wicked and evil lives. They were men who stood almost alone in facing generation after generation of unbelief and rebellion against God. They were men of heroic faith.

2 (11:33–34) **Faith, Reward:** there was the reward of heroic faith.

1. Heroic faith conquered kingdoms. This is clearly seen in the heroic faith of the leaders above. The point is this: true faith in God will stir God to give the victory over all enemies, no matter how formidable. God will even work miraculously to deliver the person or people who truly believe Him.

> **Through you we push back our enemies; through your name we trample our foes. (Psa. 44:5)**

> **Righteousness exalts a nation, but sin is a disgrace to any people. (Prov. 14:34)**

> **And we know that in all things God works for the good of those who love him, who have been called according to his purpose. (Rom. 8:28)**

> **Who shall separate us from the love of Christ? Shall trouble or hardship or persecution or famine or nakedness or danger or sword? No, in all these things we are more than conquerors through him who loved us. (Rom. 8:35, 37)**

> **No temptation has seized you except what is common to man. And God is faithful; he will not let you be tempted beyond what you can bear. But when you are tempted, he will also provide a way out so that you can stand up under it. (1 Cor. 10:13)**

> **But thanks be to God, who always leads us in triumphal procession in Christ and through us spreads everywhere the fragrance of the knowledge of him. (2 Cor. 2:14)**

> **For everyone born of God overcomes the world. This is the victory that has overcome the world, even our faith. Who is it that overcomes the world? Only he who believes that Jesus is the Son of God. (1 John 5:4–5)**

> **He who has an ear, let him hear what the Spirit says to the churches. To him who overcomes, I will give the right to eat from the tree of life, which is in the paradise of God. (Rev. 2:7)**

> **He who has an ear, let him hear what the Spirit says to the churches. To him who overcomes, I will give some of the hidden manna. I will also give him a white stone with a new name written on it, known only to him who receives it. (Rev. 2:17)**

> **To him who overcomes and does my will to the end, I will give authority over the nations— (Rev. 2:26)**

> **He who overcomes will, like them, be dressed in white. I will never blot out his name from the book of life, but will acknowledge his name before my Father and his angels. (Rev. 3:5)**

> **Him who overcomes I will make a pillar in the temple of my God. Never again will he leave it. I will write on him the name of my God and the name of the city of my God, the new Jerusalem, which is coming down out of heaven from my God; and I will also write on him my new name. (Rev. 3:12)**

> **To him who overcomes, I will give the right to sit with me on my throne, just as I overcame and sat down with my Father on his throne. (Rev. 3:21)**

> **He who overcomes will inherit all this, and I will be his God and he will be my son. (Rev. 21:7)**

2. Heroic faith ruled with justice. This means two things.

⇨ When the leaders above believed God, righteousness was produced in their lives. Faith always produces righteousness in the life of the believer.

⇨ When the leaders above believed God, they set a dynamic example of righteousness and they taught and preached righteousness. As a result, some people turned to God and began to live righteously themselves. Faith—even if it is the faith of only one person—always stirs others to believe God and to live righteously themselves.

> **Through the blessing of the upright a city is exalted, but by the mouth of the wicked it is destroyed. (Prov. 11:11)**

> **Righteousness exalts a nation, but sin is a disgrace to any people. (Prov. 14:34)**

> **Kings detest wrongdoing, for a throne is established through righteousness. (Prov. 16:12)**

> **Remove the wicked from the king's presence, and his throne will be established through righteousness. (Prov. 25:5)**

> **In righteousness you will be established: Tyranny will be far from you; you will have nothing to fear. Terror will be far removed; it will not come near you. (Isa. 54:14)**

> **Blessed are those who hunger and thirst for righteousness, for they will be filled. (Matt. 5:6)**

> **For I tell you that unless your righteousness surpasses that of the Pharisees and the teachers of the law, you will certainly not enter the kingdom of heaven. (Matt. 5:20)**

> **Come back to your senses as you ought, and stop sinning; for there are some who are ignorant of God—I say this to your shame. (1 Cor. 15:34)**

> **Stand firm then, with the belt of truth buckled around your waist, with the breastplate of righteousness in place, (Eph. 6:14)**

> **Filled with the fruit of righteousness that comes through Jesus Christ—to the glory and praise of God. (Phil. 1:11)**

3. Heroic faith obtained promises. God did just what He had promised to each of the leaders above. He always fulfills His promises to everyone who believes Him. And note: just as with each of the leaders above, He gives the assurance that He will fulfill His promises.

> **Yet he [Abraham] did not waver through unbelief regarding the promise of God, but was**

strengthened in his faith and gave glory to God, being fully persuaded that God had power to do what he had promised. (Rom. 4:20–21)

For no matter how many promises God has made, they are "Yes" in Christ. And so through him the "Amen" is spoken by us to the glory of God. (2 Cor. 1:20)

Since we have these promises, dear friends, let us purify ourselves from everything that contaminates body and spirit, perfecting holiness out of reverence for God. (2 Cor. 7:1)

Through these he has given us his very great and precious promises, so that through them you may participate in the divine nature and escape the corruption in the world caused by evil desires. (2 Pet. 1:4)

And this is what he promised us—even eternal life. (1 John 2:25)

This is the confidence we have in approaching God: that if we ask anything according to his will, he hears us. And if we know that he hears us—whatever we ask—we know that we have what we asked of him. (1 John 5:14–15)

4. Heroic faith shut the mouths of lions. This was true of Samson (Judg. 14:5–6), David (1 Sam. 17:34–35), and Daniel (Dan. 6:22). The meaning for believers is this: God has the power to control the animals and nature of this world if believers will trust God. And even more importantly, God will deliver believers from the mouth of the lion which is Satan.

Cast all your anxiety on him because he cares for you. Be self-controlled and alert. Your enemy the devil prowls around like a roaring lion looking for someone to devour. Resist him, standing firm in the faith, because you know that your brothers throughout the world are undergoing the same kind of sufferings. (1 Pet. 5:7–9)

The Lord will rescue me from every evil attack and will bring me safely to his heavenly kingdom. To him be glory for ever and ever. Amen. (2 Tim. 4:18)

And free those who all their lives were held in slavery by their fear of death. (Heb. 2:15)

If this is so, then the Lord knows how to rescue godly men from trials and to hold the unrighteous for the day of judgment, while continuing their punishment. (2 Pet. 2:9)

For we do not have a high priest who is unable to sympathize with our weaknesses, but we have one who has been tempted in every way, just as we are—yet was without sin. Let us then approach the throne of grace with confidence, so that we may receive mercy and find grace to help us in our time of need. (Heb. 4:15–16)

Let us draw near to God with a sincere heart in full assurance of faith, having our hearts sprinkled to cleanse us from a guilty conscience and having our bodies washed with pure water. Let us hold unswervingly to the hope we profess, for he who promised is faithful. (Heb. 10:22–23)

5. Heroic faith quenched the fury of the flames. This probably refers to the three Hebrew young men—Shadrack,

Meshack, and Abednego—who refused to worship the state religion of Nebuchadnezar. Therefore, they were to be executed by being burned alive. However God saved them by performing a most fantastic miracle: He preserved them and kept the flames of fire from burning them (Dan. 3:17–27).

God is God. He can preserve a person through both the furious flame of temptation and trial and the furious flame of persecution. In fact, God can preserve a person through anything. But note the prerequisite: faith in Him. We must believe God, really believe Him.

The Lord will rescue me from every evil attack and will bring me safely to his heavenly kingdom. To him be glory for ever and ever. Amen. (2 Tim. 4:18)

The LORD commanded us to obey all these decrees and to fear the LORD our God, so that we might always prosper and be kept alive, as is the case today. (Deut. 6:24)

Love the LORD, all his saints! The LORD preserves the faithful, but the proud he pays back in full. (Psa. 31:23)

For the LORD loves the just and will not forsake his faithful ones. They will be protected forever, but the offspring of the wicked will be cut off; (Psa. 37:28)

For he guards the course of the just and protects the way of his faithful ones. (Prov. 2:8)

So do not fear, for I am with you; do not be dismayed, for I am your God. I will strengthen you and help you; I will uphold you with my righteous right hand. (Isa. 41:10)

Even to your old age and gray hairs I am he, I am he who will sustain you. I have made you and I will carry you; I will sustain you and I will rescue you. (Isa. 46:4)

This is what the LORD says: "In the time of my favor I will answer you, and in the day of salvation I will help you; I will keep you and will make you to be a covenant for the people, to restore the land and to reassign its desolate inheritances. (Isa. 49:8)

6. Heroic faith escaped the edge of the sword. David escaped the sword of Goliath (1 Sam. 17:49–51); Elisha escaped the sword of the king of Israel (1 Ki. 6:30–31). Prophet after prophet was delivered from martyrdom time after time by the power of God.

God will deliver the believer from violence and death unless God wills to use the martyrdom of the dear child as a testimony and wills to take His dear child on home to be with Him. God is able to deliver the person who truly believes Him. But remember: without faith in God, no person is delivered by God. Faith is the power that takes hold of the hand of God and brings about deliverance.

But not a hair of your head will perish. (Luke 21:18)

That is why I am suffering as I am. Yet I am not ashamed, because I know whom I have believed, and am convinced that he is able to guard what I have entrusted to him for that day. (2 Tim. 1:12)

Who through faith are shielded by God's power until the coming of the salvation that is ready to be revealed in the last time. (1 Pet. 1:5)

To him who is able to keep you from falling and to present you before his glorious presence without fault and with great joy— (Jude 1:24)

Since you have kept my command to endure patiently, I will also keep you from the hour of trial that is going to come upon the whole world to test those who live on the earth. (Rev. 3:10)

For the eyes of the LORD range throughout the earth to strengthen those whose hearts are fully committed to him. You have done a foolish thing, and from now on you will be at war." (2 Chr. 16:9)

The angel of the LORD encamps around those who fear him, and he delivers them. (Psa. 34:7)

He will cover you with his feathers, and under his wings you will find refuge; his faithfulness will be your shield and rampart. (Psa. 91:4)

As the mountains surround Jerusalem, so the LORD surrounds his people both now and forevermore. (Psa. 125:2)

7. Heroic faith brings strength out of weakness. Every one of the leaders above sensed unworthiness and weakness in serving God, but God strengthened them to conquer all the enemies and forces that stood against them.

"Woe to me!" I cried. "I am ruined! For I am a man of unclean lips, and I live among a people of unclean lips, and my eyes have seen the King, the LORD Almighty." (Isa. 6:5)

"Ah, Sovereign LORD," I said, "I do not know how to speak; I am only a child." (Jer. 1:6)

But God chose the foolish things of the world to shame the wise; God chose the weak things of the world to shame the strong. (1 Cor. 1:27)

But he said to me, "My grace is sufficient for you, for my power is made perfect in weakness." Therefore I will boast all the more gladly about my weaknesses, so that Christ's power may rest on me. That is why, for Christ's sake, I delight in weaknesses, in insults, in hardships, in persecutions, in difficulties. For when I am weak, then I am strong. (2 Cor. 12:9–10)

8. Heroic faith grows powerful in battle. True faith develops and stirs courage and strength. The person who truly believes in God knows that God is with him. He is actually stirred to fight and fight, even against unbelievable odds.

It is God who arms me with strength and makes my way perfect. He trains my hands

for battle; my arms can bend a bow of bronze. (2 Sam. 22:33, 35)

Be strong and courageous. Do not be afraid or terrified because of them, for the LORD your God goes with you; he will never leave you nor forsake you." (Deut. 31:6)

"Be strong and courageous, because you will lead these people to inherit the land I swore to their forefathers to give them. (Josh. 1:6)

Joshua said to them, "Do not be afraid; do not be discouraged. Be strong and courageous. This is what the LORD will do to all the enemies you are going to fight." (Josh. 10:25)

"Be very strong; be careful to obey all that is written in the Book of the Law of Moses, without turning aside to the right or to the left. Do not associate with these nations that remain among you; do not invoke the names of their gods or swear by them. You must not serve them or bow down to them. But you are to hold fast to the LORD your God, as you have until now. "The LORD has driven out before you great and powerful nations; to this day no one has been able to withstand you. One of you routs a thousand, because the LORD your God fights for you, just as he promised. (Josh. 23:6–10)

Be strong and let us fight bravely for our people and the cities of our God. The LORD will do what is good in his sight." (1 Chr. 19:13)

Then you will have success if you are careful to observe the decrees and laws that the LORD gave Moses for Israel. Be strong and courageous. Do not be afraid or discouraged. (1 Chr. 22:13)

David also said to Solomon his son, "Be strong and courageous, and do the work. Do not be afraid or discouraged, for the LORD God, my God, is with you. He will not fail you or forsake you until all the work for the service of the temple of the LORD is finished. (1 Chr. 28:20)

I will not fear the tens of thousands drawn up against me on every side. (Psa. 3:6)

Though an army besiege me, my heart will not fear; though war break out against me, even then will I be confident. (Psa. 27:3)

You will not fear the terror of night, nor the arrow that flies by day, (Psa. 91:5)

The LORD is with me; I will not be afraid. What can man do to me? (Psa. 118:6)

When you lie down, you will not be afraid; when you lie down, your sleep will be sweet. (Prov. 3:24)

Surely God is my salvation; I will trust and not be afraid. The LORD, the LORD, is my strength and my song; he has become my salvation." (Isa. 12:2)

	S. The Great Believers' Faith (Part II): An Enduring Faith, 11:35–40	put to death by the sword. They went about in sheepskins and goatskins, destitute, persecuted and mistreated—	**e.** Some were treated in the most inhuman way imaginable
1 There was the enduring faith of believers a. Some women received their dead raised b. Some were tortured c. Some endured trials of mockery, scourging, chains, & imprisonment d. Some were martyred	35 Women received back their dead, raised to life again. Others were tortured and refused to be released, so that they might gain a better resurrection. 36 Some faced jeers and flogging, while still others were chained and put in prison. 37 They were stoned; they were sawed in two; they were	38 The world was not worthy of them. They wandered in deserts and mountains, and in caves and holes in the ground. 39 These were all commended for their faith, yet none of them received what had been promised. 40 God had planned something better for us so that only together with us would they be made perfect.	**2 There was the reward of enduring faith** a. God's approval & great historic witness b. The promised Seed or Messiah & the promised land

DIVISION IV

THE SUPREME AUTHOR OF FAITH: Jesus Christ, GOD'S SON, 10:19–11:40

S. The Great Believers' Faith (Part II): An Enduring Faith, 11:35–40

(11:35–40) **Introduction:** this is the powerful picture of what enduring faith is. It is a faith that endures even martyrdom if necessary. This passage is a panoramic scene that glances back over the history of the Old Testament and highlights the enduring faith of God's people.

1. There was the enduring faith of believers (v. 35–38).
2. There was the reward of enduring faith (v. 39–40).

1 (11:35–38) **Faith—Endurance:** there was the enduring faith of believers. Note: no names are mentioned in these verses. As verse 35 indicates, they were the women and men of every day life who were not necessarily leaders, but who had one distinctive trait: they believed God and their faith in God was strong. They endured in faith no matter what attacked them. They never accepted defeat; therefore, they were never defeated. They never denied God; therefore, they were never denied by God. They never lost hope; therefore, they were never left hopeless. They endured in faith. No matter the circumstance, difficulty, threat, injury, pain, torture, or form of execution and death, they endured and held fast to their faith and profession in God.

1. Some believers—women—received back their dead, raised to life again. This is an astounding fact, that some believers could have faith strong enough to have their children raised from the dead. Yet it is true. The Old Testament gives two examples; perhaps there were others, but they are not recorded in the Scripture (1 Ki. 17:17–24; 2 Ki. 4:18–37). In the New Testament Christ raised several people from the dead (cp. Mt. 9:18–34; Lk. 7:11–17; Jn. 11:41–46). The point is this: enduring faith—faith that will not let God go—will conquer anything including death. It is not the normal experience for God to raise people from the dead, but He has done it, and He did it because the mothers (and fathers) believed God. If they had not believed God, nothing would have ever happened. They would have just resigned themselves to the death. But they believed God and God raised them. Why? Why these

few isolated instances? Why would God raise these and not raise others? Does this mean that some had weak faith and some had strong faith? No, not necessarily. The faith of some persons, of course, is stronger than the faith of others. But some have sought God with just as strong a faith as others, yet they received a different answer. Their dead children were not raised. Why?

⇨ Because circumstances were different. God could teach them more about Himself by strengthening them to go through the death and circumstances. In addition, their testimony to a lost and unbelieving world would sometimes be stronger by experiencing the sorrow and grief of death.

We must always remember that God knows best, even in the death of children. He knows how to make us stronger and how to bear a strong testimony to the world through all the circumstances of life, even through death. But note: God cannot strengthen us, raise the dead, nor do anything else apart from faith—faith that endures. We must believe in God and His power and love, and we must endure in that belief. It was enduring faith that caused these women to receive back their dead, raised to life. And it will be enduring faith that will cause us to receive the provision of our needs from God.

2. Some believers were tortured, refusing to deny God. The word "tortured" (etumpanisthesan) means to beat or club to death or else to be put on the rack in order to make a person deny Christ. These dear believers suffered martyrdom for the name of Christ. *They refused to accept deliverance.* All they had to do was renounce Christ, but they refused. And note why: "that they might gain a better resurrection." They had their eyes on the *promised land* of heaven and glory, of living forever and ever with God and Christ. They knew something that was critical, something that is critical for every person to know:

⇨ If they had denied their faith, they would have saved their lives upon earth for a few days, perhaps even for several more years. But eventually they would have died anyway—accident, disease, old age, or something would have consumed their body and snatched or drained the life out of it.

But not faith in God. God gives life—life eternal—to the soul of man. And these dear believers were not about to turn back and reject eternal life just to walk in this evil and dying world for a few more days or at most a few years. They had their eyes on a better resurrection and world—on the resurrection and world that is eternal, never ending, and that is with God and Christ forever and ever.

3. Some believers endured trials of mockings, scourgings, and being chained and imprisoned.

- They were jeered: ridiculed, insulted, treated with contempt, and cursed.
- They were flogged: beaten with rods, whips, and cords of leather straps with bone and metal chips tied to the end—beaten until they died or were near death.
- They were chained hand and foot, sometimes for years (even Paul the apostle suffered this as well as so many of the other trials mentioned throughout this section).
- They were imprisoned in the most horrendous dungeons or prisons in the history of men.

They suffered for their faith, refusing to deny God and Christ and the glorious hope of the *promised land*—of living forever and ever with God.

4. Some believers were martyred for their faith.

- Some were stoned to death. They were thrown to the ground and surrounded by a mob of executioners. The executioners took hand size stones and hurled them at the victim causing whatever excruciating pain they could to the vital parts of the person's body and then eventually crushing the head. (Cp. Zechariah, 2 Chron. 24:20f.)
- Some were sawed in two. Oliver Greene says the method used was to put a person in a hollow log and then to saw through the log and the person (*The Epistle of Paul the Apostle to the Hebrews*, p. 514).

These are horrible pictures of death, but they are just some of the ways the world in its madness against believers have slaughtered them for their faith. Note: the believers were "lured with tempting offers [to renounce their faith]" but they refused (Amplified New Testament). They chose to receive the eternal life of God rather than a few days upon this evil and dying world.

5. Some believers were treated in the most inhuman ways imaginable.

- They were stripped of all clothing and forced to wander about in sheepskins and goatskins.
- They were stripped of all possessions—had everything taken away and confiscated—their homes, property, money, everything. They were left utterly destitute and they were afflicted and tormented as much as possible as object lessons in order to stop anyone else from believing in God and Christ.
- They were forced to wander about and find shelter wherever they could: in deserts, in mountains, and in the dens and caves of the earth.

But note the glorious declaration of Scripture: the world was not worthy of these precious people—the dear, dear believers who honored and worshipped God. The idea is this: the unbelievers of the world stripped them and confiscated everything that was *worth anything* on this earth. But the world—the whole world with all its people and all their wealth—was *not worthy* of a single one of these dear believers.

> "Blessed are you when people insult you, persecute you and falsely say all kinds of evil against you because of me. (Matt. 5:11)
>
> All men will hate you because of me, but he who stands firm to the end will be saved. (Matt. 10:22)
>
> And everyone who has left houses or brothers or sisters or father or mother or children or fields for my sake will receive a hundred times as much and will inherit eternal life. (Matt. 19:29)
>
> For we who are alive are always being given over to death for Jesus' sake, so that his life may be revealed in our mortal body. (2 Cor. 4:11)
>
> For it has been granted to you on behalf of Christ not only to believe on him, but also to suffer for him, (Phil. 1:29)
>
> Brothers, as an example of patience in the face of suffering, take the prophets who spoke in the name of the Lord. (James 5:10)
>
> If you belonged to the world, it would love you as its own. As it is, you do not belong to the world, but I have chosen you out of the world. That is why the world hates you. (John 15:19)
>
> "If the world hates you, keep in mind that it hated me first. If I had not come and spoken to them, they would not be guilty of sin. Now, however, they have no excuse for their sin. (John 15:18, 22)
>
> In fact, everyone who wants to live a godly life in Christ Jesus will be persecuted. (2 Tim. 3:12)
>
> They will treat you this way because of my name, for they do not know the One who sent me. (John 15:21)
>
> They will put you out of the synagogue; in fact, a time is coming when anyone who kills you will think he is offering a service to God. They will do such things because they have not known the Father or me. (John 16:2–3)
>
> Remember the words I spoke to you: 'No servant is greater than his master.' If they persecuted me, they will persecute you also. If they obeyed my teaching, they will obey yours also. (John 15:20)
>
> "All this I have told you so that you will not go astray. They will put you out of the synagogue; in fact, a time is coming when anyone who kills you will think he is offering a service to God. They will do such things because they have not known the Father or me. I have told you this, so that when the time comes you will remember that I warned you. I did not tell you this at first because I was with you. (John 16:1–4)
>
> So that no one would be unsettled by these trials. You know quite well that we were destined for them. (1 Th. 3:3)
>
> Do not be surprised, my brothers, if the world hates you. (1 John 3:13)

Dear friends, do not be surprised at the painful trial you are suffering, as though something strange were happening to you. But rejoice that you participate in the sufferings of Christ, so that you may be overjoyed when his glory is revealed. If you are insulted because of the name of Christ, you are blessed, for the Spirit of glory and of God rests on you. (1 Pet. 4:12–14)

2 (11:39–40) **Faith—Reward:** there was the reward of enduring faith. The reward was twofold.

1. All the believers of the Old Testament obtained a good report and testimony. Their faith touched both God and man. Their faith was the light of the world; their lives pointed men to God, and their testimonies still do. Note: their faith touched God so much that He has recorded it forever in this chapter of Hebrews. And although their names are not mentioned for the world to honor, what is important *is stressed*, that is, their faith. It is not their names that would stir people; it is their faith. It is the faith of their lives that touches the hearts and lives of people. Their faith touches people of every generation and stirs them to be men and women of stronger faith. What a legacy to leave behind, a legacy of faith that stirs and encourages people to arise and trust God and to live righteously and godly and to make this a much better world for God.

First, I thank my God through Jesus Christ for all of you, because your faith is being reported all over the world. (Rom. 1:8)

Everyone has heard about your obedience, so I am full of joy over you; but I want you to be wise about what is good, and innocent about what is evil. (Rom. 16:19)

This is what the ancients were commended for. (Heb. 11:2)

2. They had the glorious hope of *the promised land and the promised seed*. They died without receiving the promised seed. They never saw Christ born, crucified, resurrected, and exalted to the right hand of God the Father. They never saw their salvation secured by Christ, who was the very Son of God. They never saw the promise of the Messiah fulfilled. They died believing the promise, but they never knew exactly how their salvation was to be arranged.

But this is not true with us: we know. Christ has come; He has died and been resurrected and exalted to make all believers perfect and presentable to God the Father. The Old Testament believers looked forward to the Messiah; we look back upon Him. We are far more privileged. It has already happened; it is a historic fact: Christ Jesus our Lord has now died and been resurrected to make us all acceptable to God. All believers—both Old and New Testament believers—are covered by the death and resurrection of Jesus Christ. Faith in Him causes God to count us righteous and free from the guilt and judgment of sin. And being free of sin makes us perfect in God's eyes. But we must always remember: our righteousness and our perfection is in *Christ and in Christ alone*.

"For God so loved the world that he gave his one and only Son, that whoever believes in him shall not perish but have eternal life. For God did not send his Son into the world to condemn the world, but to save the world through him. (John 3:16–17)

Therefore, since we have been justified through faith, we have peace with God through our Lord Jesus Christ, (Rom. 5:1)

If you belong to Christ, then you are Abraham's seed, and heirs according to the promise. (Gal. 3:29)

It was not through law that Abraham and his offspring received the promise that he would be heir of the world, but through the righteousness that comes by faith. For if those who live by law are heirs, faith has no value and the promise is worthless, (Rom. 4:13–14)

By faith Abraham, when called to go to a place he would later receive as his inheritance, obeyed and went, even though he did not know where he was going. By faith he made his home in the promised land like a stranger in a foreign country; he lived in tents, as did Isaac and Jacob, who were heirs with him of the same promise. For he was looking forward to the city with foundations, whose architect and builder is God. (Heb. 11:8–10)

All these people were still living by faith when they died. They did not receive the things promised; they only saw them and welcomed them from a distance. And they admitted that they were aliens and strangers on earth. People who say such things show that they are looking for a country of their own. Instead, they were longing for a better country—a heavenly one. Therefore God is not ashamed to be called their God, for he has prepared a city for them. (Heb. 11:13–14, 16)

But you have come to Mount Zion, to the heavenly Jerusalem, the city of the living God. You have come to thousands upon thousands of angels in joyful assembly, (Heb. 12:22)

For here we do not have an enduring city, but we are looking for the city that is to come. (Heb. 13:14)

But the day of the Lord will come like a thief. The heavens will disappear with a roar; the elements will be destroyed by fire, and the earth and everything in it will be laid bare. Since everything will be destroyed in this way, what kind of people ought you to be? You ought to live holy and godly lives as you look forward to the day of God and speed its coming. That day will bring about the destruction of the heavens by fire, and the elements will melt in the heat. But in keeping with his promise we are looking forward to a new heaven and a new earth, the home of righteousness. (2 Pet. 3:10–13)

Then I saw a new heaven and a new earth, for the first heaven and the first earth had passed away, and there was no longer any sea. (Rev. 21:1)

PURPOSE STATEMENT

LEADERSHIP MINISTRIES WORLDWIDE

exists to equip ministers, teachers, and laymen in their understanding, preaching, and teaching of God's Word by publishing and distributing worldwide *The Preacher's Outline & Sermon Bible*® and related **Outline Bible Resources**; to reach & disciple men, women, boys and girls for Jesus Christ.

MISSION STATEMENT

1. To make the Bible so understandable – its truth so clear and plain – that men and women everywhere, whether teacher or student, preacher or hearer, can grasp its message and receive Jesus Christ as Savior, and…

2. To place the Bible in the hands of all who will preach and teach God's Holy Word, verse by verse, precept by precept, regardless of the individual's ability to purchase it.

The **Outline Bible Resources** have been given to LMW for printing and distribution worldwide at/below cost, by those who remain anonymous. One fact, however, is as true today as it was in the time of Christ:

THE GOSPEL IS FREE, BUT THE COST OF TAKING IT IS NOT

LMW depends on the generous gifts of believers with a heart for Him and a love for the lost. They help pay for the printing, translating, and distributing of **Outline Bible Resources** into the hands of God's servants worldwide, who will present the Gospel message with clarity, authority, and understanding beyond their own.

LMW was incorporated in the state of Tennessee in July 1992 and received IRS 501 (c)(3) non-profit status in March 1994. LMW is an international, nondenominational mission organization. All proceeds from USA sales, along with donations from donor partners, go directly to underwrite translation and distribution projects of **Outline Bible Resources** to preachers, church and lay leaders, and Bible students around the world.

LEADERSHIP MINISTRIES WORLDWIDE

Publishers of Outline Bible Resources

- **THE PREACHER'S OUTLINE & SERMON BIBLE®** (POSB) • KJV – NIV

NEW TESTAMENT

Matthew 1 (chapters 1–15)
Matthew 2 (chapters 16–28)
Mark
Luke
John
Acts
Romans

1 & 2 Corinthians
Galatians, Ephesians, Philippians, Colossians
1 & 2 Thessalonians, 1 & 2 Timothy, Titus, Philemon
Hebrews, James
1 & 2 Peter, 1, 2, & 3 John, Jude
Revelation
Master Outline & Subject Index

OLD TESTAMENT

Genesis 1 (chapters 1–11)
Genesis 2 (chapters 12–50)
Exodus 1 (chapters 1–18)
Exodus 2 (chapters 19–40)
Leviticus
Numbers
Deuteronomy
Joshua
Judges, Ruth
1 Samuel
2 Samuel

1 Kings
2 Kings
1 Chronicles
2 Chronicles
Ezra, Nehemiah, Esther
Job
Psalms 1 (chapters 1-41)
Psalms 2 (chapters 42-106)
Psalms 3 (chapters 107-150)
Proverbs
Ecclesiastes, Song of Solomon

Isaiah 1 (chapters 1-35)
Isaiah 2 (chapters 36-66)
Jeremiah 1 (chapters 1-29)
Jeremiah 2 (chapters 30-52),
　Lamentations
Ezekiel
Daniel, Hosea
Joel, Amos, Obadiah, Jonah,
　Micah, Nahum
Habakkuk, Zephaniah, Haggai,
　Zechariah, Malachi

Print versions of all Outline Bible Resources are available in various forms.

- **The Preacher's Outline & Sermon Bible New Testament — 3 Vol. Hardcover • KJV – NIV**
- ***What the Bible Says to the Believer* — The Believer's Personal Handbook**
  11 Chs. – Over 500 Subjects, 300 Promises, & 400 Verses Expounded - Italian Imitation Leather or Paperback
- ***What the Bible Says to the Minister* — The Minister's Personal Handbook**
  12 Chs. - 127 Subjects - 400 Verses Expounded - Italian Imitation Leather or Paperback
- **Practical Word Studies In the New Testament** — 2 Vol. Hardcover Set
- **The Teacher's Outline & Study Bible™ - Various New Testament Books**
  Complete 30 - 45 minute lessons – with illustrations and discussion questions
- **Practical Illustrations — Companion to the POSB**
  Arranged by topic and Scripture reference
- **What the Bible Says About Series – Various Subjects**
- **OBR on various digital platforms**
  See current digital providers on our website at www.outlinebible.org
- **Non-English Translations of various books**
  See our website for more information or contact our office

— Contact LMW for quantity orders and information —

LEADERSHIP MINISTRIES WORLDWIDE or Your Local Christian Bookstore
1928 Central Avenue • Chattanooga, TN 37408
(423) 855-2181 (9am – 5pm Eastern) • FAX (423) 855-8616
E-mail - info@lmw.org • Order online at www.lmw.org

www.ingramcontent.com/pod-product-compliance
Lightning Source LLC
Chambersburg PA
CBHW080216040426

42331CB00035B/3114